SHORT-BALLOT PRINCIPLES

INSTRUCTIONS TO VOTERS:

Where a party has made no nomination for an office, the space for that office is in the voting circle under the party heading.

It a party ticket does not contain the names of candidates for all offices for which the voter may vote, he may, if he votes the straight ticket of such party, vote for candidates for such offices by writing the names of such candidates under the title of the office. To vote for a person not on the ballot, or in case of erasure, change the title of the office, write the name in the blank column.

ALL MARKS EXCEPT THE CROSS (X) ARE FORBIDDEN. ALL DISTINGUISHING MARKS OR ERASURES ARE FORBIDDEN AND MAKE THE BALLOT VOID. If you WRONGLY STAMP, TEAR, or DEFACE THIS BALLOT, return it to the Inspector of Election and obtain another.

REPUBLICAN TICKET	DEMOCRATIC TICKET	INDEPENDENCE LEAGUE TICKET	SOCIALIST TICKET	PROHIBITION TICKET	INDEPENDENT NOMINATIONS	GOOD GOVERNMENT ORGANIZATION TICKET	BLANK COLUMN	CONSTITUTIONAL AMENDMENTS AND PROPOSITIONS

A LONG BALLOT (LOS ANGELES, CAL.) AND A SHORT BALLOT FROM ENGLAND

The Californian ballot (original size 23 × 32 inches) is no longer than that of several other states, Colorado, Ohio, or Illinois, for example

SHORT-BALLOT PRINCIPLES

BY

RICHARD S. CHILDS

BOSTON AND NEW YORK
HOUGHTON MIFFLIN COMPANY
The Riverside Press Cambridge
1911

COPYRIGHT, 1911, BY RICHARD S. CHILDS

ALL RIGHTS RESERVED

Published September, 1911

TO

THE AMERICAN PEOPLE

WITH THE ASSURANCE THAT THEY ARE

NOT TO BLAME FOR THEIR MISGOVERNMENT

THIS VOLUME

IS LOYALLY DEDICATED

PREFACE

WHILE I entitle this book "Short-Ballot Principles" I am aware that it contains a number of things which are only remotely connected with the Short-Ballot movement. Short-Ballot advocates are justified in asking: "'The Wieldy District' idea, the 'Leadership Parties,' and 'Nomination by Forfeit' — are *these* Short-Ballot principles?"

No. The title is meant to cover only those chapters which deal with the Short-Ballot principle as defined by The Short-Ballot Organization; which is: —

First: That only those offices should be elective which are important enough to attract (and deserve) public examination; and,

Second: That very few offices should be filled by election at one time, so as to permit adequate and unconfused public examination of the candidates.

But the Short Ballot, far reaching and important as it is, will not completely answer present difficulties of self-government. "New York City practically has the Short Ballot," says a doubter; and I must explain that the mere bigness of the electoral district creates a special problem which the Short Ballot does not answer, and that big cities must have the *right kind* of Short Ballot, else the "machine" will stay and prosper. So likewise to answer other critics I must talk of parties and of nomination procedure and get those things into the same perspective as the rest of the book. But these postscripts are only my personal answers, and any Short-Ballot advocate is free to differ and to offer other reasoning of his own without impairing his orthodoxy!

RICHARD S. CHILDS.

New York, February, 1911.

CONTENTS

I. Our Political Superstitions and the Scientific Spirit 1

II. Democratic Government has Limitations 10

III. The Short Ballot 21

IV. The Office must be Important 31

V. The Nature of Popular Interest . . . 43

VI. The Limit of District-Size 51

VII. Fits and Misfits 59

VIII. Ramshackle Government 119

IX. Parties and Why they cannot be Responsible 130

X. "Leadership Parties" 144

XI. Nomination Procedure 154

XII. Conclusion 162

L'Envoi 170

SHORT-BALLOT PRINCIPLES

CHAPTER I

OUR POLITICAL SUPERSTITIONS AND THE SCIENTIFIC SPIRIT

My purpose is to present in these pages a view of democratic government from a distance not usually taken by American citizens, — a distance so remote from the whole tangle of reasoning as to cast into clearer perspective the meaning and relation of the various parts.

In considering the problems which we have met in the course of our adventure in democracy, we Americans have very rarely stopped to take a look at the whole proposition of popular government. We have wrestled with functions instead of causes. As a nation we have never been more than merely superficial in our theories of political science.

In fact, most Americans seem unaware that there *is* such a thing as political science. Any sensible lawyer is considered competent to draft a plan of government for a city. Honesty qualifies a business man to go to a state constitutional convention. In talking to miscellaneous audiences on subjects of this nature, I have been repeatedly secretly amused at the easy nonchalance with which men who had never before given a thought to the problems of governmental organization would wave aside statements quoted from such men as ex-Presidents Eliot of Harvard and Woodrow Wilson of Princeton, as if there could not possibly be any elements in democratic problems that were not visible to any amateur at a glance. The only parallel I know of is the profession of advertising. Almost any average man thinks himself competent to write good advertisements without any study or experience, and every advertising agent earns his commissions ten times over in squelching the foolish proposals of his clients.

And so when a council proves corrupt, our city charter is merely amended to transfer the control of contracts to a new board of public works. If the state surveyor is untrustworthy, we create a new official to build the new canal. If the county clerk makes his office a feeding trough of patronage, we create a civil-service board to supply him with an eligible list. New York takes the control of franchises away from the aldermen as a measure of reform while Chicago (as a measure of reform) is adding to the powers of its aldermen — and in both cases reform is for the moment achieved, since corruption is a plant that often takes more than a moment to grow in new environments. So we go on, doctoring symptoms instead of looking for the disease!

In fact, in any tentative exploration in the direction of fundamentals we have been stopped time and again by certain widespread political superstitions among our people — superstitions that usually have as their nucleus an ancient catch-phrase. Propose that a mayor be allowed a seat and vote in the council, and the proposal will be heard on its merits until some one says: "That violates the principle of the *'separation of powers.'* There you have legislative and executive functions united"; and with the advent of the catch-phrase, it is deemed the duty of the proposer to bow in awed silence, as if the argument were ended. Propose to make the state engineer appointive, on the ground that the plan of having him elective has worked badly, and the word "*undemocratic*" falls like a gavel to end the discussion. Plead that a referendum on a technical subject is little better than leaving the decision to chance, and the query, "*Don't you trust the people?*" is supposed to retire you in confusion. Robert Louis Stevenson was right when he said "Man shall not live by bread alone, but principally by catch-phrases."

That in our political reasoning we should be the slaves of these glib "bromidioms" is probably because the subject is the common property of the millions. Any idea that is to be widely spread and remembered must be condensed to a catch-phrase first, even if such reduction means lopping off many of its vital ramifications and making it false in many of its natural applications. A dozen well-chosen words can travel from mouth to mouth great distances and keep their alignment unbroken; but make the phrase longer and it falls apart and stops, — or only a fragment of it travels on.

The power of these catch-phrases to sway men's minds, regardless of reasoning, is a fascinating thing to see. The Des Moines plan of city government at this writing is winning favor with thousands because they say it is "a business form of organization," — just "like a corporation with its board of directors," — although in fact it is really like a board of department superintendents elected by the stockholders, — a form of organization unknown in business and never likely to find favor in business practice. If it were really like a board of directors, the "commission" would appoint a manager who in turn would hire the departmental heads, reporting regularly to the commission and submitting to it only broad matters of policy. Yet the catch-phrase has converted whole cities, while the fundamental but less catchy reasons for the comparative success of the plan have rarely been mentioned!

In this volume I propose to remain at a point of view so distant that the whole network of catch-phrases will be lost sight of, and we shall see democracy as a whole, never getting close enough to see the details. If we can only keep for a while at such a distance that nothing but the fundamental features will be visible! It will be hard, but perhaps it will help if I take the liberty of warning you against the greatest catch-phrase of all — namely "the people," pronounced "pee-pul"! Or, worse yet, "the plain people," who, I believe, have certain supernatural virtues not possessed by "the people." It is *lèse-majesté* to allege that there are any limitations to the people in either morals or learning. We are only beginning to emerge from the period when thought on the question of popular government was simply used to supply the savor, and not the substance, for oratory. "Rounded periods" are out of fashion on every other subject, but rhetorical vaporings still enshroud "this great people"; and if you should have the temerity to opine that most of the people vote for a state treasurer blindly without adequate knowledge of his qualifications, a hundred editors (after having looked up the name of the state treasurer themselves to be sure of it) will explode in paragraphs of fury, inveighing against your "aristocratic sneers." In the same editorials, after exalting the intelligence and virtue of the people, I have seen them proceed to deplore the "wanton indifference of the age" and "the prevailing absence of civic energy"!

And there we have another familiar set of catch-words. "Apathy" is a catch-phrase, and I shall show you later that the notion that "our people are apathetic toward their political interests and duties" is one of our political superstitions. I shall be a long way on with you, Mr. Citizen, if I can persuade you—

First, that the people are men and women — not demigods.

Second, that the people are men and women — not moral delinquents.

If we thus concede to the people the faults and merits possessed by men and women, we can proceed calmly to consider them as the great underlying force of democratic government, with certain well-known and, so far as we are concerned, unalterable characteristics to be reckoned with as we erect the political superstructure.

Think of the people as you would of water when building a water-mill! You would waste no time in deploring its lazy tendency to slip downward through every crevice in your dam — you would admit the fact and build a tight dam. You would not plan to have the water flow uphill, knowing that you would inevitably be disappointed. If your mill finally failed to work, you would still not blame the water but only the mill, and would strive to adapt its gearing to the force of the stream. Yet you would have just as much right to sit by the motionless mill and curse the characteristics of water (which consistently fails to fulfill your man-made requirements) as has the Charter-Revision Committee to devise a city charter that imposes requirements on the people which ample experience demonstrates that the people will not fulfill, and to curse the people for failure to live up to these arbitrary "duties."

So in this volume I shall try to get you to consider "the people" in the same scientific spirit in which you would consider the water, ascribing to them no unnatural virtues, no powers that have not been revealed in practice, no halo, no golden glory; to consider them as a phenomenon of nature which in a given set of circumstances will do certain things and will not do certain other things.

In the past we have approached the people as a pagan approached the waterfall — to worship and peer around for nymphs. We must to-day approach the people as the mill-builder approaches the waterfall, open-eyed, unafraid, expecting no miracle, measuring its capacity, making allowance for its variations, and irreverently gauging its limitations in order that our mill shall not exceed them. We shall learn perhaps that the "crystal drops" contain a certain percentage of sediment, that though the stream "goes on forever" it goes rather slowly in a dry summer, and that the "resistless force which cuts the stern granite and yet makes way for a baby's hand" amounts to just a certain horse-power and can be trusted to saw just so many feet of lumber per day.

In considering the people in this scientific, unpoetic spirit we shall not, I promise you, become cynics. The engineer who reduces the waterfall to a sheet of mathematics has just as real a respect for it as the sentimentalist who writes a rhapsody to it. I hope to land you safely in the last chapter possessed of a discriminating admiration for our American people in politics, freed from vague mental reservations and fears, with an unclouded optimism, and a faith that involves no mysticism, but is comfortably established on a foundation of frank reasoning.

CHAPTER II

DEMOCRATIC GOVERNMENT HAS LIMITATIONS

Now I will suppose that the previous chapter has gotten us into the coldly scientific and unsentimental state of mind where we can safely trust ourselves to measure and calculate the various elements of popular government without danger of either magnifying or ignoring any of the features we see.

The problem before us is:—

Given the American people,

How to organize among them a government which in all normal times will be impelled promptly and intelligently to learn their desire and perform it.

This does not mean merely that the government will obey on those occasions when the people in a paroxysm proclaim from press, pulpit, and mass meeting that a certain thing must be done (though even that would be substantial gain in some American communities). It means a government which is so sensitive to the currents of public opinion that it will even *anticipate* the popular wish.

DEMOCRATIC GOVERNMENT

There is nothing fanciful in such an ideal. Commerce is no less sensitive than that. Every taste of the public in food, art, and comfort is catered to without any conscious public inquiry for such satisfaction. It is profitable to our purveyors to please us with new dainties for the table, comfortable shoes, pretty homes, and records of Caruso's voice. Rarely do we as a people need to express a want for such things — the knowledge that we shall like them is enough to stimulate their production. So in our ideal democracy we shall want something better than legislatures that say, "Yes, that's a good idea, but there's no public demand for it," as if the fact that they had not yet been kicked were satisfactory excuse for inaction! Rather we want legislatures that will even surprise us with good things that most of us had not yet had time to hear agitated, — knowing us and knowing what we like, each public servant racing to be the most popular and to win our bestowal of honor and office by inventing new political delights!

Democratic government is government controlled by the people, and has three important variations of form.

First: the town meeting where the people

themselves gather in conference and, after debate, decide for themselves upon their laws and communal activities. The average man will readily agree that this form of democratic government is only suitable in a limited field of application and is unpractical in large cities, or sparsely settled communities of large area, or communities where the governmental activities are complex and technical in their nature.

Second: the referendum, wherein laws are devised by some committee, official or otherwise, and submitted for approval to popular vote. The average man will readily agree that this form of democratic government also has its limits of practicability and that, for instance, to have *all* the laws of a state made in that fashion would be quite out of the question.

Yet what would happen if some limitations of these forms of democratic government were ignored? Suppose Chicago were forced by the terms of an ancient village charter to submit its vast governmental activities to the tender mercies of an annual public meeting of all the citizens! Of course all the citizens could not get into a single hall nor within sound of a single voice, and the few thousand who could do so by trick or violence could gain control and keep it

DEMOCRATIC GOVERNMENT 13

year after year. That would be oligarchy, — the rule of the few, — although any politician armed with a few carefully selected catch-phrases could indignantly argue that it was exactly the same form of government which, when used in New England towns, had proven a triumph of pure democracy! Inasmuch as it looked as if it *ought* to be a democracy, thousands of citizens would actually believe that it must be one and that the true remedy for the resultant ills of the system lay in "more civic virtue," "a more militant good citizenship," and "the education of the people" so that they wouldn't shout and yell so at the meeting. If you asserted that the overstepping of the limit of practicability in the size of the electorate had been in itself sufficient to alter the whole principle of the plan, making it normally and naturally productive of violent oligarchy instead of democracy, you would be called an "academic aristocrat," "distrustful of the pee-pul," or a "dilettante who disliked to jostle in the rough mob!"

Does the picture of such stupid opposition seem overdrawn? Wait. It is actually the present condition of American political thought, except that I have imagined it applied to the town-meeting form, instead of to the third form of democratic government, namely *government by elected officers.*

Government by elected officers, which of course is by far the most important of the three typical mechanisms for ascertaining and executing popular will, is supposed to work as follows : —

It is known that a certain office in the government will on a certain day be filled by popular vote. The office is made attractive by salary and honor. Several eligible men covet the position and accordingly go among the voters seeking favor. If any considerable section of the voters want a certain policy adopted in that office, either the need of securing their support will lead candidates to announce concurrence in that desire, or the opportunity to obtain office by means of their support will produce new candidates who do concur in it. Thus, any important demand among the people is automatically reflected in the list of candidates whose names appear on the ballot on election day. Then the voters go to the polls, and knowing which candidate best represents their individual desires, they mark his name on the ballot. The officer thus elected is the one who has successfully catered to the wishes of the greatest

DEMOCRATIC GOVERNMENT 15

number. The necessity that every elected officer shall thus find favor with the people, gives the people ultimate control.

That is the theory. We are so far from it in practice that it has a strange look. It is a sound workable theory nevertheless. But it has its limitations, just as town-meeting democracy has. And if these limitations are overstepped, oligarchy automatically results.

Some of these limitations are merely mechanical; others are rooted in human nature itself.

The mechanical limitations do not commonly bother us much, for they are easy to see and hence are unlikely to be overstepped. For instance, the polling-place must be orderly. If it be unguarded by the police, the opportunity to capture an election by violence will be left open to any group of ruffians, and it is a reasonable certainty that some group of ruffians will sooner or later perceive and grasp the opportunity. "Bleeding Kansas" before the Civil War was the unhappy scene of just such occurrences. The rule of the few (oligarchy), instead of democracy, the rule of the many, is thus the logical, normal, inevitable result of a failure to observe *this* limitation of democracy by election.

The most familiar illustration of overstepped mechanical limitations is in the form of the ballot and the method of marking it. The rules governing the voter in the act of voting must be simple and easy to comprehend. Tricky arrangements of the ballot or intricate rules of procedure may operate to disfranchise thousands of voters. The operation of voting might easily be made so elaborate that the bulk of the people would be certain to violate the rules and lose their votes — and again, government by a small minority would result automatically.

Notice that in such cases the failure of democratic government to develop according to programme is only the normal, to-be-expected result and implies no discredit whatever to the people. The people are the same under an unpractical form of democracy as under a practical one.

It would be easy to invent a thousand ways of planning an apparently democratic form of government that would in all normal conditions result in oligarchy. Knowing that the people are obliged by natural economic pressure to work to their maximum efficiency at gainful occupation, it is only necessary somehow to elaborate electoral processes until the bulk of the people haven't time to master those processes — whereupon they automatically become the political slaves of those who do have time.

Suppose, for example, that the polls, instead of being placed at every barber's shop, were placed in the centre of the county, so that the bulk of the people had to travel considerable distances to get there. Suppose also that elections came every month instead of once or twice a year. Sheer inability to spend so much time on their unpaid duties of citizenship, when these interfered with the nearer duty of getting bread and butter, would automatically exclude the majority and throw control of the government into the hands of those few who lived near the polls. That would, of course, be oligarchy; yet again the catch-phrase makers could argue that it was genuine democracy. It could be argued that the people had the right to vote but were defaulting their obligations, and we should hear of the need for "an aroused civic conscience" and "an awakening of the people to their privileges." Men of easy conscience would take up their residence near the polls for the sake of the opportunities there, while men in that locality who were unwilling to misuse those opportunities would have less incentive than the latter to remain in the neighborhood and would tend to be forced out. The group of voters near the polls would be holding the government in an informal trust for the balance of the electorate. And since that power would be accessible to any one who chose to live there, and would offer livelihood and wealth to corrupt men and nothing but thankless labor to good men, it is inevitable that the trust would be betrayed.

Would the people be to blame for not protecting their own interests under those circumstances? Could it be fairly claimed that they *ought* to give up productive labor on so many days of the year? Is it not clear that those of the people who whole-heartedly strove to fulfill these arbitrary requirements of citizenship would suffer in business competition with those who did not? Should the merchant close his shop so that he could go to vote, leaving his less patriotic competitor in possession of the field? Would not the clerk who insisted on taking a day off every month to vote be worth less to his employer than one who was willing to ignore such "duties"? Would not the first question asked of an applicant for a job be: "Do you insist on voting?" The conditions would put a

DEMOCRATIC GOVERNMENT 19

premium on the neglect of politics. None but the independently wealthy or the unemployed could afford to be factors in the government without remuneration. And it would be no reflection on the people if it were found that only a few were in politics — rather it would show that they were loyal to the higher duty of working as hard as they could to provide home and comfort for their families.

The whole outcome of a failure to keep within this limitation of "convenience of voting" can thus be easily seen to be wholly irrespective of the "civic virtue" of the people. It is an outcome that would result among peoples which now govern themselves with complete success, as certainly as among peoples whose self-government is commonly characterized as rotten.

Now for the rule based on this reasoning. (Look out! For if you are so incautious as to admit this point, I shall have converted you to the major premise of this whole book.)

No plan of government is a democracy unless on actual trial it proves to be one. The fact that those who planned it *intended* it to be a democracy and could argue that it *would* be one if the people would only do thus and so, proves nothing — if it doesn't "democ," it isn't democracy!

And I will ask you to agree as a result of this chapter of fancies, that democracy has limits, — many limits, — and that overstepping some of these limits may result in oligarchy.

From this point we will move nearer to our subject, and see whether our American form of government has not at some points gone beyond the limits of practicability.

CHAPTER III

THE SHORT BALLOT

GETTING a government that will normally obey the people is a matter of making it feasible for the people to put into public office the men they want there — and none else. This, in turn, is a matter of exposing candidates to adequate public examination before election, so that when the voters go to the polls they will have had ample information to enable them to decide intelligently which man they want as their representative and servant.

If after the people have seen a man they elect him, they must stand by their verdict. Their only protection is to see what they are getting. The only thing that can happen is that they may elect a man they do not really want, and that sometimes happens. The only legitimate protection the people may be given is the fullest chance to scrutinize the candidates. Arrange for the fullest, most intensive scrutiny, and you have done all that can be done. Scrutiny at election is vital to democracy. Deny to the people the opportunity to scrutinize the candidates, and you have left them fighting blindly and futilely in the dark.

One method of concealing the candidate from the public gaze is to have so many elections at one time that each candidate is sheltered by the confusion.

Notice I use the plural — "elections." The habit of saying "election day" instead of "elections day," and "election" instead of "elections," has caused more trouble than any other idiom of the language. When we fill ten offices by popular vote in a single day, we call it "an election," but it is really ten elections.

When Ohio holds forty-seven elections on one day, does the average citizen read the names, casting a straight Republican ticket only when finding that each Republican candidate is to his liking? Or does the average citizen ignore the individual names for the most part and place his dependence on the party management? To find this out, demand of the average citizen on the evening following elections day, as he stands before the stereopticon screen watching the returns, "Whom did you vote for?"

"Taft for president and Harmon for governor," he will answer.

THE SHORT BALLOT

"Whom else?"

"The Republican National ticket and the Democratic State ticket."

"But what men? You voted for forty-seven, you know, and you've only named two! Whom did you vote to send to the state legislature? And whom did you pick for county clerk? And for dairy and food commissioner and coroner?"

"Oh, I don't know — I'm not in politics."

I dare say that even the politicians of Ohio take most of their ticket on faith in this way.

In Cleveland a certain militant reformer relates that he spent most of his time for weeks before one of these elections working as one of a committee to investigate all the candidates and publish recommendations for the guidance of the voters. He had special facilities, he became an expert in the business of citizenship, and by election time was one of the few men in town who had studied all the candidates of all parties. When he went to vote, himself, he found to his dismay that he had omitted to bring along his carefully compiled memoranda. He attempted to vote for the long list of forty-seven offices from memory, found himself confused and in doubt at various points, and finally cast a ballot which he later found contained several mistakes.

In giving weeks of time to political inquiry, this man was doing no more than every citizen was supposed to do. If he needed a memorandum to aid his memory, it is reasonable to suppose that every other citizen needed one at least as badly. If the citizens knew what they were doing at that election, every one of them must have had such a memorandum in the polling-booth, copying the forty-seven separate marks, the vote must have shown substantial variations on different offices, and the citizens must have been exchanging ideas for many days beforehand on such subjects as Smith's qualifications for the post of state dairy and food commissioner, and Jones's ideas regarding the administration of the coroner's office! Did they? Or did the citizens vote without stopping to read the ballot, without knowing even the names of all the offices that were to be filled, simply rubber-stamping, without scrutiny, the ready-made tickets of the politicians? And if the politicians are only ten per cent or five per cent, or, as I suspect, less than one per cent of the population, is not Ohio an oligarchy?

When the ballot is long, *i. e.*, when there are many offices to be filled simultaneously by popular vote, the people (except in village elections where they can recognize every name at sight) will not scrutinize every name, but will give their attention to a few conspicuous ones and vote for the others blindly. In voting blindly for any name the politicians select, the people are simply delegating their choice to a few half-known, irresponsible men whom they had no voice in choosing. The attempt to get the people to say who shall be county clerk, for instance, has failed. It is like asking a question of a crowd and accepting the few scattering answers as the verdict of the whole mob. It is not democracy, but oligarchy, just as in the imagined case of a county that held incessant elections at an inconvenient polling-place. In this case it is not the inconvenience of *voting* which practically disfranchises the bulk of the citizens, but the inconvenience of *voting intelligently*. In the test of practice it has thus been demonstrated that if the people are asked forty-seven questions at one time, they will not give back forty-seven answers of their own, but will let others make most of these answers for them.

This is no reflection on the morals or intelligence of the people. (Even if it were, in planning a workable democracy we should have to cut our cloth accordingly.) It is simply evidence that there is such a thing as asking the people more questions than they will answer carefully. In blindly ratifying party nominations the people of Ohio are doing a much better thing than voting at random or not voting at all. The controlling elements in the party have some slight responsibility and some desire to "make good." There is some chance to blame and punish some one if things go wrong.

Let us imagine a typical citizen trying to do better, — trying to get along without party guidance, — trying to act as an independent judge, without bias and thinking only of the common good. His vital need is for light on the subject. How is he to get it? Remember that economic pressure is driving him to his maximum efficiency in gainful occupation. To do his duty to self and family he must work as hard as he can. If he finds himself still fresh at the end of the day's labor, it signifies that he could safely have worked harder or longer to give his wife a better home or his children a better education! Any unremunerated labor that he expends displaces profitable labor and can be performed only in small amounts or for short periods. Sustained effort in unpaid work, whether it be the work of citizenship or something else, is incompatible with his economic efficiency. For the average man, pressed by competition in mill or shop or office, it is simply impossible.

To "go into politics," to become an active and responsible and effective force in a political machine, is utterly beyond the powers of the average man, because it calls for a very large amount of such sustained unpaid effort. For the most part the men who are active in politics are not unpaid. Either their political acquaintance is in some way profitable to them or they are chronic office-holders who regard political activity as part of their job. (Young men with energy to spare and no family burdens are also frequently seen in such circles; but when they marry and begin to feel the economic pressure they soon retire from active work.)

Yet to "go into politics," impossible as this generally is, is the only way our typical citizen can gain any direct information regarding the men on whom he is to pass judgment at the polls. His newspaper barely mentions the candidates for minor offices — its limelight flits over them fitfully, and finding nothing picturesque, leaves them in darkness. Candidates sometimes campaign and get elected on the tail of the ticket without ever getting a line of newspaper publicity. They can get no individual hearing because the public is hardly aware that their little office is being contested for. A candidate for clerk of courts who tried to explain to the people the work of his office and the improvements he proposed to install, would be classed as "eccentric" and his efforts would be futile. This or that audience might listen respectfully enough, but he could never force the issue to a point where his opponents would feel obliged to reply. Forty-seven elections does not mean forty-seven technical debates during the campaign, by any means. The people, unable to oversee so many separate contests, simply allow sets of candidates to be tied together for them in bunches like asparagus, and then vote them by the bunch. A hopeful independent candidacy in Ohio for one of these minor offices is almost unheard of. An independent contestant would be utterly lost in the shuffle and could not secure any public attention.

All the power of public discussion is so wasted by dissipation that our typical citizen is unable to hear enough facts to obtain basis for a judgment. It is no disparagement of the comprehension of the average citizen of Ohio to say that he never casts a completely intelligent ballot — it is only saying that, being a man, and not a cat, he cannot see in the dark!

Thus the sheer amount of political work thrust on the Ohio citizen is so great that he cannot perform it intelligently without the impossible sacrifice of economic efficiency. The typical Ohio citizen, therefore, wisely defaults these excessive political obligations which are thus arbitrarily put upon him, leaving the control in the hands of those few who for one reason or another can take time and energy for such work. A ballot of forty-seven offices thus makes citizenship a specialty — a profession — a thing for experts and not for the people.

If forty-seven places is too long, then how much shorter must the ballot be?

If the people are not to rely blindly on ready-made lists prepared for them, they must rely on individual lists of their own. That fact reduces us to the psychological question: How many candidates will the average man remember for himself? How many separate contests will he keep clearly defined in his memory? How many mental images or impressions of contesting candidates will he hold in mind without confusion? For on election day he is to see their names before him on the ballot, and to choose for himself on a basis of his knowledge regarding them.

Exact determination of the number is not possible, but the best test is to observe the tendency of "tickets" to appear when a non-partisan ballot is in use. We are near enough now to the end of the problem to establish a rule: —

To keep a government by elected officers from becoming an oligarchy, —

The ballot must be short!

How short?

Short enough (!) — so that the number of choices to be made by the voters will not be so great as to conceal the individual candidates from a public scrutiny that will be adequate to exclude any one whom the voters do not really want.

CHAPTER IV

THE OFFICE MUST BE IMPORTANT

I LEFT you in the last chapter with a formula on your hands instead of the answer itself. My reason was that in any examination of facts regarding the trouble caused by overlong ballots, we find the evidence inextricably entangled with a second cause of invisibility — namely, the unimportant character of many elective offices.

We might have a short ballot that covered only one office; but if that office were that of coroner, the people at large would shrug their shoulders and pass on indifferent. There are and ought to be other things more important to the people than the question, "Who shall be coroner?" It is no slight thing to ask all the men of a city to bestir themselves all at one time regarding *any* question. The question may easily be too trivial. The average man's share of interest in getting the better candidate for coroner elected is so infinitesimal as not to warrant the slightest exertion on his part. The powers of the coroner in a small community are insignificant. In a large city the coroner may have a busy office, but in proportion to the community he is insignificant still. If ninety per cent of the people are indifferent to the issue, the remaining ten per cent will have their way in the matter — and there we have a bit of oligarchy. If the coronership were the only office to be filled on a certain day, only a few of the people would go to the polls, and the attempt to make the people stand up and be counted on the issue would thereby be a failure. If the mayor and the coroner were the only two offices to be filled, the people would be drawn to the polls by the mayoralty contest, but their votes on the coronership would represent no clear or adequate information and would be easily influenced by the few citizens who were interested. A full vote for coroner under these circumstances would be no more a real verdict of the people than in the other case.

Probably no city has suffered so much from ballots that ask fatuous questions as Philadelphia. A few years ago I was invited to address a luncheon at the Philadelphia City Club, a political-reform association, and was

OFFICE MUST BE IMPORTANT 33

astonished to find that the Saturday selected for the discussion of my purely academic subject was the one immediately preceding the Tuesday of a semi-annual election — a time when it would be expected that the "burning issues of the campaign" would be the natural theme. But neither the city streets nor the club-house showed anything to indicate that an election campaign was in progress. The local newspaper of that Saturday contained only one column of political news — a statement issued by the "Committee of Seventy," which began, "We beg to remind (!) the citizens of Philadelphia of the election to be held next Tuesday." Members of the City Club who had been enough interested in better government to come to the luncheon to discuss civic problems said that they did not know what officials were to be elected or who the candidates were. The absence of newspaper publicity and general interest made it probable that the rest of the city knew as little. An examination of the ballot gave an ample answer for the condition. None of the offices were of importance, being minor judicial and clerical posts; and the city of Philadelphia, in wasting little attention on the election, was relegating the whole issue to its proper position.

One of the elective offices, for instance, is that of inspector of election — the officer who is to count the votes at the polling-place. The incumbent works only one day. There are 1170 of these posts in Philadelphia. If all their work were concentrated in one officer's hands it would not, even then, make a conspicuous office. How inconspicuous it becomes when subdivided into 1170 parts was revealed a few years ago when one "Clarence Boyd," who was elected by "the triumphant verdict of the people," was some time after discovered to be non-existent. (The man who appeared and performed his duties came from outside the state, so that when wanted later by the courts on account of frauds which he perpetrated while in office, he was not obliged to go to the inconvenience of changing his domicile!)

Now this is an extreme case, to be sure — but it is a real one, and as we can ofttimes comprehend an extreme case more clearly than an ordinary one, we will use it as a text.

In theory the people of Clarence Boyd's district should have studied the relative qualifications of the various candidates and chosen the

OFFICE MUST BE IMPORTANT 35

one who met with their approval. In a community where no man knew all his neighbors, however, the fact that Clarence Boyd did not exist was not discoverable by the methods of inquiry that are available to the average voter. The fact that there was absolute silence on the part of Clarence Boyd during the weeks prior to election excited no suspicion. Candidates for the office in question never make a campaign, for the ample reason that no one would ever listen if they did. Nothing but the discovery of a plot for fraud would attract attention to such a picayune contest.

Now the Committee of Seventy investigates these little nominations, to point out the reliable candidates. Many people when they understand the plan follow these recommendations. They will not do so on account of evidence submitted to them, but primarily because the Committee of Seventy wants them to, and they trust the sincerity and the ability of that organization. The publication of the name of the candidate recommended, unaccompanied by evidence, is enough for practically all the voters who accept this leadership. This is a vital point! Open-eyed acceptance of leadership is legitimate and desirable; but here we have blind acceptance — an entirely different thing, for it gives the leaders opportunity to profit by misleading their followers. Open-eyed acceptance of leadership involves few perils; blind acceptance involves many.

When the office is sufficiently uninteresting, it becomes invisible, and the popular acceptance of leadership will then be blind.

The ways in which a ballot may be uninteresting are numerous. In the Philadelphia instance just cited, the office was too miserably insignificant to stir the multitude to adequate inquiry. Many offices lie outside the purifying spot-light by reason of their character, even when they are of considerable importance. Technical offices, for instance, are habitually in obscurity, and the same is true of any clerical or purely administrative post. What, for instance, can the candidate for the post of state treasurer do to demonstrate his superiority over rival claimants for the position? He can claim that he will be honest and systematic and intelligent — but so can his rivals. If the accounting system of the state is out of date he can promise reform — but he can't stir the people to strenuous partisanship on his behalf by talking about book-keeping. Nothing

OFFICE MUST BE IMPORTANT

he can do can alter the fact that there is little or nothing in the state treasurership out of which to make an issue that will fire the imagination of a million voters. There is an inevitable loginess to the mass of the people — the simple inertia of bigness. Let our candidate talk to a quiet little audience of a hundred, and he will win them. Let him talk to an audience of several thousand, and he will be unable to hold their attention at all on such a subject. His appeal to the million will fall flatter yet; in fact, he will secure no hearing at all. Accordingly such candidates habitually ignore their own contests and confine themselves to supporting the head of the ticket and the broad party issues of the campaign.

Looking at the matter from another angle, suppose that the Republican and Democratic candidates for state treasurer in New York were nothing more than respectable politicians. Would that fact create opportunity for an expert accountant to run independently for the place? Would the fact of his superior fitness be enough to make New York's eight millions look his way and make note of him for election day? Theoretically, yes. In fact, no. Independent candidatures for such offices in states and cities are quite unknown and unhopeful. In a court-room an interesting case obtains fair hearing from the jury because the jury must stay and listen; but here are advocates pleading their uninteresting case before a crowd in the market-place, the crowd being at liberty to drift away to the ball game if it chooses! The case will be decided by the few who remain — oligarchy again!

Any office which may properly be conducted in only one way will make an uninteresting subject for an election contest. The people cannot be expected to take sides on a question if it is only a one-sided question. Partisanship cannot be provoked when all the rival candidates promise the same things. Unless a conspiracy to misuse the office can be alleged (and not always then), the people will not develop a preference among the candidates. The difference in the lives and equipment of candidates will rarely come clearly enough before the millions to make them divide on these personal distinctions alone. The question of which man shall draw the salary is not momentous and cannot be made so.

Into this classification of undebatable offices

OFFICE MUST BE IMPORTANT

fall many that are now elective in the United States. To retain them on the elective list is undemocratic. Nothing is so undemocratic as government in the dark, and to put on the elective list offices which are naturally and inevitably invisible is compelling the people to delegate power to officials cloaked in darkness. The more obscure the office, by reason either of its insignificance or of its undebatable character, the weaker is the control of the people over it, and the stronger is the control of the politician.

The net result of all these considerations is to show a need for the elimination from the elective list of

(1) all offices that are not large enough in themselves to stir the people to take sides;

(2) all offices that determine no policies large enough to stir the people to take sides.

For if the people won't settle the question you put to them, some few self-seekers will. To shout at the people questions which the people either will not or cannot answer carefully, is not doing the people a favor. It is only making certain that the questions will be answered by some one else.

We must confine the participation of the

people to questions which they want to decide. *Each elective office must be interesting.*

The test to apply to an office to ascertain whether it is "interesting" is, of course, to inquire whether it does actually interest the people. Your opinion or mine as to whether the office of judge *ought* to interest the people is of no importance; the question is — *Does* it? If the bulk of the people are interested enough to divide on the question and stand up and be counted on the issue, then the judge may properly be made elective. If only a few of the people develop opinions clear enough to impel them to take sides in the contest, then your plan of having all the people select the judge has failed to work. You have created oligarchy instead of democracy. You must then make the judge appointive by some one whom the people did select.

By taking sides, I do not mean merely that the people must vote. Goodness knows, the people will vote readily enough without taking sides! A full vote for the city clerk does not mean that the whole city, or any perceptible part of it, was really interested. Look closely at the vote and you will notice that the city treasurer was elected by practically exactly

OFFICE MUST BE IMPORTANT

the same majority as the clerk. Look back over the records of previous elections and you will find that one year the two Democrats were elected by parallel pluralities and next year the two Republicans were elected also by almost identical figures. How curious that each time the two candidates of one party should find favor with almost the same number of people! The absence of wide fluctuations is one proof that the people did not really take sides at all, but blindly delegated the work *en bloc* to their party managers.

Another way to investigate is to inquire, as in the case of the long ballot discussed in the previous chapter, whether the voters know what they are doing on election day. If most of them can give no reason for preferring Smith over Jones as city clerk, then obviously they are not doing the selecting, but are blindly ratifying some one else's selection for that office. Democracy requires that all the people shall join in doing the selecting. To make them do the electing is by no means sufficient.

The people must take an interest in all their electoral work if they are to be masters. If they do not take an interest in a given ballot there are two solutions — change the people or change the ballot. As the people are too big to be spanked, and since human nature in the mass responds but slowly to prayer, it is good sense to change the ballot.

Don't forget our major premise — if it does n't "democ," it is n't democracy!

CHAPTER V

THE NATURE OF POPULAR INTEREST

DEMOCRATIC government is government controlled by the people, and all the real rights of the people are served if the government obeys their wishes. If the wish of the people is unanimous, and if the government acts in accord therewith without waiting for orders, an election is unnecessary. An election is due whenever the people are interested in a question and divided in their opinions. A democratic government will then arrange to have the people stand up, divide, and be counted, and being unable to please all, will be content to please the majority.

For example, it was proposed a few years ago in New York State to enlarge the Erie Canal at a cost of $101,000,000. Vast interests were affected, whole cities expected renewed prosperity from it, yet the cost was enormous. The legislature did not know the feeling of the people on the subject. The matter was put before the people by referendum and the expenditure was authorized. The selection of an engineer to construct the canal was not however a matter of sufficient interest to the people to warrant the taking of a vote. Everybody wanted the work done well, economically, and promptly, but was perfectly willing to let the governor appoint the engineer. Had the engineer been made elective, the people would have been confronted with a task of the utmost delicacy, — not a task where the opinions of the multitude were of value, but one which demanded intensive and intimate investigation, such as could be conducted only by a very few men. It is no easy task to choose an engineer for such a great undertaking. The task calls for special information rather than the collection of many judgments. The appointive way which was adopted secured for the people better service than the elective way.

The choice of a good administrator is an even more delicate task than the choice of a good engineer. An engineer can point to definite achievements and evidences of standing in his profession. He can say: "I built that bridge — does not that prove me competent to take charge of public works? My rival has never built a bridge, nor can he attain in private practice fees half so large as mine." But an executive must be selected on less tangible evidence, and his work in office is harder to appraise with justice. Business corporations pay their biggest salaries to good administrators for ability to initiate, to be just, to inspire loyalty in subordinates, to avoid errors, to see things in true proportion. Success in such things cannot be measured and tabulated. Only men close at hand, where they can see it, can judge it wisely.

Even the stockholders of a corporation do not pledge their directors to support any given candidate for general manager of the company. They get better results by leaving the decision to representatives who are in closer touch with the situation than they. To reorganize the corporation by making the stockholders elect the manager over the heads of the directors would not add to the power of the stockholders, since all the power comes from them anyway, and wise stockholders would resist any attempt to unload the responsibility upon them in this fashion. It would not be a privilege; it would be denial of privilege — the privilege of holding some one else accountable. So, too, the people, who are the stockholders of the state, are entitled to have the government run as they want it run, without having to leave other duties to take hold and run it themselves; and any attempt to throw unnecessary burdens of participation upon the electorate plays into the hands of any public employee who wants to evade responsibility.

To relieve the people of the burden of choosing administrators would liberate public discussions from a mass of dull detail that obscures greater issues. The principles proposed by the candidate should not be entangled with evidence as to his fitness for personally administering the execution of those principles.

The real interest of the people in the government is not in administrative problems, but is in making the government obey when they desire to issue an order. Their interest is in policies, and usually the easiest way to put policies into effect is to elect men who are charged with the spirit of those policies to positions where they can compel the installation of the new ideas.

Popular control over policies is not difficult to provide for. The people may be too big and clumsy to handle the delicate task of choosing administrative officials, but there can be no

NATURE OF POPULAR INTEREST 47

doubt of their ability to sympathize with this or that proposed policy and to determine which candidate represents their favorite ideas. The candidate who thus wins people to his proposal may not be the one who can best carry them out. But he may wisely be put where he can issue the mandate and compel obedience.

In one of the commission-governed cities recently a labor-union man was elected a member of the Commission of Five to govern the town. He had two separate duties — to represent the people who elected him and to administer the department of parks and public property. As a representative of the great laboring population he was admirable. He could say with real authority: "My people want to have push-carts allowed around the factories at noon so that they can buy cheap coffee and fruit for luncheon, and I'm against an ordinance to clear the push-carts off the streets. Put on extra men to clear up if necessary."

It was right that labor should thus be represented in the high councils of the city. Every important section of the people should be represented in its due proportion in the government. Democracy demands it.

As administrative head of the department

of public property, however, this man was ineffective. Administrative work was foreign to his experience and abilities. He was displaced at the next election in favor of a business man, and his people lost all representation on the Commission.

This was both wrong and unnecessary. The office should have been divided according to its administrative and representative functions. The administrative office should have been appointive, the representative, policy-determining office alone should have been elective.

The removal of all offices from the ballot except those purely representative ones that interest the people on account of the broad policies which they may determine, will take us a long way towards the "interesting" ballot we are looking for, but not all the way.

To take an exaggerated case again, look at the lower house of the Philadelphia councils. It determines policies and interesting ones, too. But it contains 149 members. Its decisions are futile unless approved by the other council and by the mayor. The choice of a single member of this house is not a big enough matter by itself to excite the interest of the people, and so Philadelphia is called "corrupt and con-

NATURE OF POPULAR INTEREST 49

tented." Interest can be subdivided until it is not interest at all.

Accordingly, to conform to the rule that "the office must be interesting," we find that each elective office must have a *large* effect upon interesting policies.

How large?

Large enough (!), so that its importance will induce the people to look after it.

To depart from this rule involves serious diminution of public interest, and the office sinks back out of the spot-light of public scrutiny and becomes invisible and beyond popular supervision. When the people delegate power to an *unseen* officer they lose control of that power, and the government ceases to be at that point a government controlled by the people — ceases, that is, to be a democratic government.

Democracy requires that the power shall not pass out of sight of the people, but shall remain entirely within their vision, in the hands of visible officers.

Safety demands also that the power shall not be delegated to too *few* officials, lest the people become victims of personal official caprice; but the power must on no account be subdivided and scattered so widely that the individual officers, by reason of their unimportance, lie outside the borders of the spot-light. Concentrated *visible* power is controllable and not dangerous. Our visible elective servants will never become our monarchs — it is our invisible servants who organize oligarchies and monarchies of bossism!

To summarize the last three chapters, then, we find that there are three practical methods of concealing public servants from their masters, the people, and thus causing popular control to relax: —

(*a*) By having so many elections simultaneously that each individual candidate is lost in the confusion;

(*b*) By dividing a power among so many petty officers that each one of them escapes scrutiny by reason of insignificance;

(*c*) By making an office undebatable in character, so that discussion regarding it is dull and unlikely to attract attention.

Condensing this to a catch-phrase, we establish what we will call the First Limitation of Democracy: *Each elective office must be visible.*

CHAPTER VI

THE LIMIT OF DISTRICT-SIZE

HAVING simplified the work of the people to a point where they need no help from political experts in casting their votes, we have not yet got the power completely into their hands. The short, interesting ballot is not enough if the only names on that ballot are those nominated by political machines. To be sure, the fact that the nominations are to be exposed to the searching light of concentrated public scrutiny will compel the machines to be deferential to public opinion. Tammany nominates reputable men from outside its own ranks, even borrowing them from the reformers' ticket, for the conspicuous offices. But even if the limitations of democratic government described in the previous chapters were fully observed, a Tammany Hall would continue to be a necessary part of the government of New York City. Imagine all the power put in the hands of the board of estimate, with its three members elected at large and one from each borough. Each citizen votes for four members only. This means a short, interesting ballot that fulfills all the requirements laid down in the preceding chapters, each elective office playing a large part in determining interesting policies. Then imagine the idea adopted that is in effect in Colorado Springs and elsewhere, of not only having no party labels on the ballot but making every candidate, when filing his petition, swear that he represents no political organization or club! In the little city of Colorado Springs the requirement works perfectly. In the city of New York that plan would limit the candidates to millionaires. None less could finance a campaign designed to reach 600,000 voters. The expense of hiring halls in all parts of the city, drawing the crowds to the meetings, advertising in circulars or newspapers and on billboards, would, if this work were adequately done, be enormous — much greater than it is now, when the ability of the machines to throw into the field a vast standing army of well-trained volunteers cuts down the money cost. A candidate could spend $100,000 without even making a serious dent in the consciousness of the big town.

LIMIT OF DISTRICT-SIZE

Making the multitude listen, making them all think about the same thing, is a task that becomes more difficult the larger the multitude. The discouragement of candidates and the consequent serious limitation of possible contestants is not the most serious disadvantage of big electorates. Suppose all the political machines of New York City gracefully retired from the field, leaving all contestants on an equal footing. One candidate or another would build up a *personal* machine equipped by experience and funds to win elections for him. The superior effectiveness of such methods in a huge population would put a premium upon evasion of all laws seeking to prevent the existence of political machines. These armies of political mercenaries would drift from one leader to another, seeking the highest pay, and their organized coöperation, formal, informal, or secret, would be vital to the success of the candidates. No candidate could build up such an army of political workers at short notice or with genuine volunteers who expected no reward. (The "volunteers" in the present machines are really paid by preference in political appointments and city jobs where the hours are short enough to permit steady political work.)

All this is only saying that large electorates are hard of hearing, and they can be so large as to be almost deaf. This deafness of a big electorate to all but expert organized political noise-makers gives to the political experts an influence which amounts to virtual control.

To express it another way, an electorate may be so large that it cannot perform even a simple task without organizing for it. A committee can easily do in half an hour the work that a convention of a thousand men can only do in a stormy, blundering fashion in a whole day. In fact, a convention can hardly get anywhere except with the aid of committees. The clumsiness of a convention is nothing to the clumsiness of a hundred thousand men scattered through a great city; and if concerted action is required of them, there must be organization. In huge electorates it will have to be a more elaborate and costly organization than we can ask the candidates to construct; and if the support of these standing armies is essential to the success of candidates, it follows logically that these armies (or the captains of them) will hold an unassailable monopoly of the hopeful nominations.

Democracy requires that there shall be rea-

LIMIT OF DISTRICT-SIZE

sonably free competition for elective offices. To give to any set of men power to exclude various candidates from the contest may often result in barring out the very men the people would like. It is not possible to suppress permanent political organizations when they will be of great help in winning the great prizes of office, but it *is* possible so to arrange the battleground that there will not be enough advantage in permanent political organizations to encourage their existence.

Let the political unit or district be not so large but that an adequate impromptu organization can be put together at short notice. Permanent committees or political organizations may then exist without controlling the situation, since the threat of opposition, if their nominations are unsatisfactory, will be truly serious. In theory, if the parties in New York City both nominated unsatisfactory men, new candidates would spring into the field and get elected, thus automatically penalizing any failure of the old machines to please the people. In fact, of course, the mere bigness of the task is enough to discourage independent candidates, and the existing machines preserve a safe monopoly over the business of nomination —

oligarchy again! In the smaller subdivisions of the city, such as the Aldermanic and Municipal Court districts, independent nominations are not infrequent, and sometimes succeed despite the fact that the offices are ones which do not naturally secure public scrutiny.

The smaller the district and the fewer the voters to be reached by the candidate, the weaker is the grip of the machine, the easier it is for the political novice to succeed, and the less is the advantage of the political specialist who "knows the ropes."

Enlarge the district beyond a certain point and the business of winning an election becomes a job for experts only; and we get, in part at least, government by politicians instead of government by the people.

Accordingly we establish the Second Limitation of Democracy: *The district must be wieldy.* Our unwieldy districts are as unique in the experience of democratic countries as are our long jungle ballots.

Granted then that New York City is too large a district, what the exact maximum is for the voting population for a "wieldy" district can be determined only by the test of practice. Regarding any existing district, the ques-

LIMIT OF DISTRICT-SIZE

tion to determine is — For a visible office (as per the First Limitation of Democracy), do the people in this district find that their choice is unduly limited by the difficulty which candidates who lack the support of standing political organizations have in getting a hearing? Or to express the same idea differently — Can a spontaneous movement of public opinion express itself without getting permission from political machines?

Political subdivisions in our cities, to be sure, have a bad name, although in the excellently governed cities of Great Britain the ward is the unit everywhere. The fault with American ward politics does not lie in the pettiness of the ward so much as in the pettiness of the powers of ward-elected aldermen. Make the alderman a big conspicuous office, and the character of ward politics would be instantly revolutionized.

The ancient minor evils of log-rolling and gerrymander must be cured in other ways than by election-at-large. In British cities, for example, the councilors elect about one third their own number (aldermen) to sit with them. These aldermen are elected for longer terms than councilors and in rotation. Having no districts, they are independent of ward influences and their presence in the council makes log-rolling awkward. Gerrymander in British cities is prevented by having the ward lines adjusted by a remote (parliamentary) authority.

Proportional representation is also offered. By that plan the district or constituency loses its boundary, so to speak, and all officers are elected at large, with this difference — that the candidates instead of being required to get a plurality need get only a quota. If ten offices were to be filled in a city of 100,000 voters, for instance, the quota would be 9091 (since not more than ten candidates could each get that number). To prevent waste of votes on candidates who get more than a quota and on candidates who prove hopelessly weak, the preferential ballot is employed, whereon the voter marks a first choice, a second choice, etc., and the ballot, in the counting, is transferred from candidate to candidate in accordance with the voter's indicated wish, until it finds a resting-place. This is the Hare or Ware system used in some of the British colonies. Its significance here is the fact that the candidate need only secure a quota instead of a plurality.

CHAPTER VII

FITS AND MISFITS

I HAVE now proved, I hope, that democracy is not a thing of magic with infinite capabilities, but that it has certain limitations which are not moral short-comings of, but only the results of the inevitable clumsiness of, that great good-hearted and human giant, the people. Among these limitations are the following, which must be respected to prevent democracy from lapsing into oligarchy.

1. *The office must be visible;* that is, it must be (*a*) not crowded out of sight by too many simultaneous elections; (*b*) not too small to be seen; (*c*) not too uninteresting in character to get looked at.

2. *The district must be wieldy.*

In our American governments, we have almost invariably overstepped these limitations, turned democracy into oligarchy and then found that oligarchic conditions furnished to the ruling class, the politicians, opportunities, too often utilized, to plunder the many.

Accordingly, let us take together a grand tour of the United States to inspect the workings of our so-called democratic governments in various places and see how they fit (or fail to fit) within our limitations.

TOWN GOVERNMENTS

In small compact communities the offices are visible and the district wieldy. The discussion in earlier chapters regarding the limitations of visibility, however, does not apply. The offices may be numerous and petty in character, but the fact that candidates are personally known to the voters contributes a unique kind of interest that makes up for other deficiencies.

Accordingly, the American town should be a democracy or else there must be other limitations not mentioned.

And is not the typical American town relatively an excellent example of democracy? There are politicians, but they are not in control as are their brothers of the cities, since any citizen can enter the field and threaten their supremacy as soon as they, by failure to bow to public opinion, give provocation. Town opinion rules town politics surely, promptly, and easily. Notice how national party symbols fail to hold the people in line on local issues, and how spontaneous, genuine caucuses and "Union Parties" take the place of the inflexible unresponsive machinery of less wieldy districts! That town government is either efficient or cheap, I do not claim. I only believe that it conforms very nearly to the civic ideals of the people who live under it and that every change in those ideals is reflected with reasonable accuracy and promptness in the town government.

GALVESTON

This city (40,000 inhabitants) was formerly governed, like most other American cities, by a mayor, a council elected by districts, and various minor elective administrative officials. Most of the offices were not visible. The members of council individually had so little to do that it was hardly worth the time of the people to bother about them, and so a few of the people who did bother took control.

The district, in the case of all the officials (including the mayor and other officials elected at large), was wieldy, since the task of reaching the voters in a city of 40,000 inhabitants is not so colossal as to suppress impromptu political movements.

And Galveston was badly governed. The power which the people delegated to their officials was not all kept in the light where the people could easily observe how it was used. When some misuse of power became known, the chance of anybody suffering political punishment was slight. All the politics concerning such obscure offices as that of member of council was beyond the vision of the people. It was not conspicuous — not placed on a pinnacle of light where they all could see it and make it a target for their criticism. Council politics, or ward politics, especially, was a thing to be searched out in the by-ways and shadows of the town. It required special knowledge and acquaintance. Who but a political expert would know, for instance, when, or over what saloon, the little conferences that really settled things would meet? What ordinary citizen working for his bread and butter in competitive industry could afford to devote to this part of the unpaid work of citizenship enough time and study to keep from being outwitted by those other citizens who were stimulated by the hope of tangible pay in patronage or boodle? The failure of Galveston to make its elective offices conspicuous had turned a large part of its politics into a veritable jungle where none but experts knew the trails. And so a handful of experts in citizenship, called politicians, ruled Galveston. Galveston was an oligarchy.

General disgust among the people of Galveston with the council led to a change in the charter, by which the council was elected at large instead of by wards. "Ward politics" was thus to be abolished. It was believed that election at large would wipe out the field for petty manipulations, log-rolling and cheap politics in the council. The new plan doubtless did change the rules of the game and demoralize the grafters for a time. Every such change seems to be a reform for a while; since corruption, even in favorable soil, is a plant of slow growth, dependent on the continuity of surrounding conditions.

Under the new plan —

1. The offices were not visible. All the members of council now appeared on all the ballots instead of singly on the ballots in each district, making the ballot much longer and the possibilities for blind voting many times greater

than before. Each member was still only a small fraction of a weak council and hence naturally inconspicuous.

2. The district remained wieldy.

In this new situation the people had no surer grip than before. Their work at the polls continued to be poorly lighted, and they fumbled and faltered in all efforts to protect their interests against the encroachments of Privilege — whether it was the privilege of a rich man to get a franchise cheaply or of a poor man to get an easy job in the City Hall. The politicians continued to rule the town — three per cent of the people ruling the remaining ninety-seven per cent. It was oligarchy — the rule of the few; unstable, loosely and informally organized, to be sure, but still an oligarchy. It would have been an oligarchy just as surely if the "reformers" had been in control, giving the people exactly the kind of economical and efficient government that was best for them. Democracy requires that the people themselves get what they want, whether in your opinion or mine it be altogether good for them or not. Effective citizenship — a very different thing from mere "citizenship" — must be for the masses, not simply for political specialists

FITS AND MISFITS 65

who know their way through the political jungle.

Galveston's mistake was in trying to get rid of the politicians without providing any substitute to do their work. Of course the only proper substitute is the people themselves. But the people cannot work in the dark — only political experts can do that — and the continued and inevitable absence of the people from the darksome scene of operations left the intricate controlling levers of the government unmanned, and liable not to be worked at all unless the volunteer specialists in citizenship had come forward.

In 1900 the waters of the Gulf of Mexico were swept by a great gale clear over the low levels of Galveston, and when they receded, Galveston was gone. Faced with great emergencies incident to reconstruction, the city government found itself inadequate and inefficient. It was never designed to act quickly or do much, anyway. Some ancient superstition — some fear of kings — had led to making the government purposely inefficient lest it become able to do harm. Thereby it became equally unable to do good. The emergency made an efficient government so supremely desirable, that for once the superstitions gave way. Galveston adopted the famous "Commission Plan," by which the entire government of the city was vested in a board of five elective officers who in turn appointed and controlled all the rest of the officials.

To Americans accustomed to inefficiency in public office as contrasted with private enterprise, the story of the achievements of this Commission reads like a romance. Unhampered by checks and balances and legal red-tape, the Commission reorganized the city government, restored the city property, planned and financed and built the great sea-wall that now bars out the sea, raised the ground level of the city, and, withal, reduced the tax-rate and the debt! The annual running expenses of the city were decreased one third. The new government displayed foresight, intelligence, and dispatch. It appeared sensitive to that public clamor which the average politician considers so needless.

There was a striking change in the attitude of the public toward the doings at City Hall. The people began to "take an interest" in their common property, to discuss the doings of the Commission on street corners, to have "civic pride" (since there was now at last something to be proud of), to criticise or applaud the work of their servants. They seemed to have actually a proprietary interest in the government! Amid this widespread discussion the influence of the politicians of the town was swamped and counted for only its true numerical strength.

Now every American city has its spells of good government, — the reactions that follow orgies of corruption and scandal, — and the fact that the new Galveston government saved money is not in itself significant. The vital difference is that these good administrators in Galveston, without building up personal "machines" or intrenching themselves in power by the usual army-like methods of political organization, were able to secure reëlection again and again. They won favor by serving all the people well. They did their work in the spot-light of public scrutiny, where every citizen could see and appreciate and applaud. There is no reward sweeter or more stimulating than well-earned public applause. Good deeds under the old government were frequent, no doubt, but in the jungle the doer received no encouragement or glory.

"By serving all the people" — not by serving a few men who occupied strategic positions in a political ambush! In fact, there was no obscuring ambush to afford opportunities for strategy. The commissioners were getting reëlected, and by overwhelming majorities, without any organized aid save the support of the City Club. The expense of reëlecting them was $350 for all five! When the people knew from their general information exactly what they wanted, why conduct a big campaign? Why try to build up a standing organization of political workers when the simple governmental plan left no work for it to do?

Let us apply our two Limitations of Democracy to the Galveston plan.

1. The officers are visible — only five to elect, all playing a large part in determining interesting policies.

2. The district is wieldy.

Perfect conformity!

OTHER COMMISSION-GOVERNED CITIES

There grew up in Galveston the custom of dividing work among the members of the Commission and letting each of the five specialize in the affairs of one branch of the government. The members did not assume executive charge of the departments, — that work was done by hired expert superintendents, — but simply became familiar with the work by observation. In fact, the commissioners remained in private business and simply gave a few hours a week to the city as needed. The public soon anticipated the organizing of the Commission, and the division of the government over which each commissioner would probably be given special oversight, became a matter of general knowledge before the election.

In copying the Galveston plan, other cities, Houston for instance, made this division formal so that each commissioner became the responsible active superintendent of a department, giving all his time to it and receiving increased pay accordingly.

The people thus have thrust upon them a more difficult task than in Galveston — namely, that of selecting the best men to do administrative work. The people have no great relish for this task, as is proved by the way in which they habitually neglect elective offices which are *purely* administrative. Moreover, it is work for which they have no great ability. The opinions of 20,000 voters on the question which of the candidates is best fitted to supervise sewerage, or paving, or the city's fiscal operations, are not valuable. If you or I were engaging an engineer for a private contracting firm, the fact that one candidate for the place had secured 10,000 votes in Houston for a similar position would carry small weight with us. We should recognize that those votes were based on hearsay evidence, not investigated for its accuracy by a dozen voters out of that 10,000. We should recognize that the popular support the candidate secured was based rather on the fact that he had satisfied those voters, that he represented them, sympathized with them, was like them, knew what policies they wanted. For his qualifications as an engineer we should prefer the report of, say, five responsible investigators.

To confound these two separate issues, fitness to represent and fitness to administer, interferes with both accurate representation and efficient administration. Perhaps Houston is electing to superintend its public works a first-class engineer who has no real intimacy with the people. Or perhaps Houston is electing a mediocre engineer who has the gift of popularity and broad comprehension of the desires of the people. The chance of getting a maximum of both desiderata is remote. The requirement of high administrative ability in elective offices makes it necessary to confine nominations to the kind of men who earn large salaries in private life and wear kid gloves. It excludes labor, for example, which is too little represented in the government of typical American cities.

Of the two things, *fitness to represent* will naturally be the dominant factor in electing a man, for in that matter there is ample ground for a debate on policies that will actually stir the people and cause them to divide. It is policies that make real politics, and the most efficient democracy is that which provides for the freest expression of the demands of the people in regard to them. Let each elective office, therefore, not only play a large part in determining interesting policies, but also be kept free of every other consideration. "When you want representation, elect. When you want administration, appoint."

The mayor of Houston was elected as a separate officer, and was given special powers and duties, including the right of veto over the acts of the Commission.

Measured by the requirements of visibility, this feature can hardly be construed as an improvement on the Galveston plan. The mayor's office is made more interesting and conspicuous, but the offices of the other four commissioners are made less so. The mayor becomes all-important at the expense of his associates, who play a much smaller "part in determining interesting policies" than in Galveston.

So far as Houston is concerned, the elevation of the mayor at the expense of his associates has done no harm and may never do any, for the harmony of the Commission is reported to be so excellent that the mayor's veto power has not been used. To a certain extent usage thus far has nullified the error in the design, and the four commissioners are regarded as highly important, and get ample limelight at the election to protect their office against capture by men whom the people really do not want.

In a certain middle-sized Eastern city there is on foot at present writing a plan for adopting a new charter in which the Houston error is carried to its logical conclusion. The plan provides for five elective officers — namely, a mayor and a council of four members. The mayor is the chief executive of the city, appoints all city employees, draws up the budget, and in general runs the city. The council has power only to stand around and watch things, to trim down the budget, but not to increase it or revise it, and to pass ordinances subject to the mayor's veto. This is perilous. There is danger that the mayor will completely overshadow the other four, and that the latter will not count for enough to attract the light. Complete ready-made tickets for the council will then automatically appear and be accepted or rejected *in toto*, without individual examination by the people, even with the non-partisan ballot that is planned; and with the makers of those tickets the people will share control over the council. The plan will result in an imperfect democracy because the ballot is four fifths uninteresting. The people will control the mayor, electing the man whom they really know they want, whereas the council will in the long run be composed of men whom the average voter cannot recall by name, men who get elected without passing through the light, men of whom it may eventually be said that they got elected without "detection." And if rascals should slip into these offices under cover of the gloom, could the people be blamed? Must they be expected to see in the dark?

COLORADO SPRINGS

In copying the Galveston plan of government, Colorado Springs has introduced a provision in the charter to the effect that every candidate, before his petition for a place on the official non-partisan ballot can be accepted, must file a sworn declaration that he represents no political party or organization. As a temporary expedient to break the grip of the old party machines this provision was apparently valuable, for the largest plurality at the first election under the new charter in this normally Republican city went to a Democrat. The permanent desirability of the measure is less certain. It is interesting, however, as showing the practicability of unaided democracy when the Two Limitations are respected. The people of Colorado Springs are dealing with their public servants directly without calling for expert assistance. The candidates make themselves known to the people, each in his own way without help from anybody save his personal following. The voters also make up their individual minds and vote without help.

The politician, in the American sense of that word, is a useless spectator with no more influence than any other citizen of wide acquaintance. He can go to his favorite candidate after election and say, "I helped elect you — therefore reward me out of the city treasury"; but he cannot say, "I helped elect you as no other citizen could — I was necessary to you, therefore reward me for permitting you to be elected."

The difference is enough to free city officials from the embarrassment of partisan machine control. To those who offer aid before election, each can say, "I welcome help but do not require it desperately, nor do I need a great deal. I can afford to refuse aid from all but those whom I can pay in cash from my own pocket or who volunteer unconditionally, and I prefer to do so." Such a statement to the politicians under old conditions would have foredoomed the candidate to defeat. The political world is full of men who have met this situation and compromised grudgingly at the ultimate expense of the public, because nothing else was "practical."

BOSTON

In January, 1910, Boston put into effect a new charter which aimed to adapt to a large city the fundamental features of the commission plan. The charter provides for a very powerful mayor elected for four years, a council of nine members (weak and obstructive) elected for three-year terms, three at a time, in rotation, and a school board (administrative) of five members elected one or two at a time for three-year terms. The ballot is non-partisan, all nominations being by petition. There are six places or less each year to be filled by popular vote from the whole city.

Measuring Boston by our Limitations, we find that the offices are not all visible. Only the mayor plays "a large part in deciding interesting policies."

The district is not wieldy.

At present writing there have been only the first two elections, and the plan has not had time to settle down to what will be its regular pace. Certain significant facts, however, stood out even at the first election with sufficient clearness to warrant interpretation and a prediction.

FITS AND MISFITS

There were four candidates for mayor who survived the rather heavy petition requirements, namely Fitzgerald, a Democratic ex-mayor, under whose former administration there had been much complaint of misgovernment; Hibbard, a Republican ex-mayor; Storrow, the nominee of a committee of reformers representing the independent good-government vote; and Taylor, apparently representing no one but himself and his prospective constituents. Taylor was out of the race from the start. It was recognized that his support was only personal, that he had no machine at his disposal to carry his message to the voters, and that there was no long-standing, well-established "good will" in his favor. Hibbard had been too rigidly scrupulous a mayor to win the admiration and zealous support of the Republican machine, but he recognized that his only hope of success lay in getting that support, and his newspaper advertisements bid for it openly and desperately, in a manner that indicated that he regarded Republican support as more precious than the good opinion of reflective voters. He did not get the Republican machine support, though the Republican politicians found it more worth their while to be active than they had at first expected. Certainly the candidates all valued their support and manœuvred for it, and the stock of the candidates rose and fell according to the rumors of their success in these flirtations. Fitzgerald had the whole-hearted though informal support of the Democratic machine, which he had richly befriended in patronage and favoritism when in office before. He was thus able to win support at much less expense than Storrow, who spent $95,000 on his campaign and gathered almost the entire anti-Fitzgerald vote. Hibbard and Taylor ended with only 1800 and 600 votes respectively.

Storrow's huge expenses are the fruit of the unwieldiness of a district as large as Boston, and show how the mere size of the task of winning over a great electorate must operate to narrow the competition to a few men, none of whom may be what the public really wants. In the future the political organizations of long standing — namely, the Democratic machine, the Republican machine, and the organized independents, with their coterie of civic workers and reformers — will hold a monopoly of the hopeful nominations. A candidate must always have the support of at least one of them in order to win. If he can secure the support of two of them he will be almost invincible. To build up *de novo* an impromptu volunteer organization capable of winning the election against the old established organizations is hardly a hopeful undertaking.

The only hope of any such movement in Boston now lies in the increased probability of a division of the party strength by factional disputes when there is no one of sufficient authority to stop the fighting. Even this chance seems on reflection somewhat remote. For suppose two candidates, equally strong among the Democratic politicians, began to claim party support. We know enough about politicians to know that they would be politic and would wait, shrewdly estimating the relative strength of the candidates until one showed a lead, whereupon they would flock to him with a rush, leaving the other to grow steadily weaker. Ordinary human desire to be on the winning side is trifling compared with that desire among politicians whose bread and butter depends upon their being there.

To believe that in the future the people of Boston will not be sharing their control over the mayor with some coterie of political specialists is to assume that the politicians will refuse to sell their support to the highest bidder, or that no candidates will bid for such support even if getting it will contribute greatly to their success.

At the second election under this charter (January, 1911) there were chosen three members of the council and two members of the school committee — a short but uninteresting ballot and an unwieldy district. On the day before the election the papers were telling who the candidates were, in a style they might be expected to use in explaining the matter to out-of-town visitors; the voters were urged to be sure to vote, the news regarding the campaign occupied a single half-column and, despite the short ballot, tickets were being advertised. There was never so dull a city election in Boston. As in the first election, all the candidates who were elected had the support of machines, and the importance of that support was indicated in the way that one candidate, for example, who had been obscure and out of the race, became suddenly an acknowledged leader the moment a certain party committee graciously issued its endorsement.

FITS AND MISFITS

Hereafter it may become more important for a candidate to get on that committee's ticket, or some other ticket, than to campaign vigorously for popular favor; and in just the ratio that this is true the people will be sharing with a coterie of ticket-makers their control over their government. If these ticket-makers win because they support candidates whom the people learn to like, their function is simply harmless leadership. If they win because the people can't see in the gloom and hence are forced to delegate their work blindly to experts in citizenship, then the ticket-makers can exercise discretion, knowing that their selections will be accepted by the people without examination. And this power, especially in the hands of political organizations which any corrupt man can join and help to direct, is a dangerous diversion of a power that should remain entirely with the people, if democracy is to be complete.

I believe therefore that Boston will find that it has not devised a practical form of democratic government.

NEW YORK CITY

New York is governed by its board of estimate of eight members, elected three at large and one from each of the five boroughs. There is also a very weak board of aldermen, elected singly from districts.

Each voter in the city votes for four members of the board of estimate, and an alderman.

In respect to the aldermen, the First Limitation of Democracy is overstepped, — the office is not interesting and hence not visible.

In respect to the board of estimate, the Second Limitation is overstepped, — the district is not wieldy, except in the case of the member from the borough of Richmond.

The borough of Richmond consists of Staten Island, a small district, suburban in character, and with a population of 100,000. It is apparently a wieldy district and thus conforms to both Limitations. Amid the bitter political warfare in the other boroughs of New York City, this little district seems to have found much the same kind of peace and stability that Galveston has. The political organization seems to have no control over the office of the borough member of the board of estimate, or "borough president" as he is called; and three times a man, who in his administration of the borough ignores the local politicians, has been reëlected over their heads. There have never been charges against him — a delightful contrast to the experiences of the other four boroughs, in all of which there has been much scandal and in two of which the borough presidents have been removed for misconduct.

The borough president of Richmond cannot claim that his good record is the result of superior moral calibre. He has been under no serious temptation. If politicians come to him demanding that some heeler be given a job, he can refuse, knowing that if they attempt to side-track him at the next election he can reach the people with his personal appeal, and even if not renominated by his party, can at least completely upset borough politics by running as an independent. So he bows the politicians out, makes appointments for merit, wins approval from his people because he is conspicuous and important enough to have his good deeds noticed, and announces himself a candidate for reëlection; and the politicians, needing him on the ticket more than he needs them, hasten to renominate him. The officer and the people are within reach of each other and the intermediation of the politician is superfluous — all because the office is visible and the district is wieldy.

The other four boroughs of the great city, Bronx, Manhattan, Brooklyn, and Queens, are decidedly unwieldy. Each has an immense population and a great area. For a single man, unaided by a big ready-made organization, to tackle the huge mob and make it notice him is out of the question.

Still more unwieldy is the city as a whole, which comprises the district of the three members of the board of estimate who are elected at large — namely, the mayor, comptroller, and president of the board of aldermen. How the mere inertia of so huge an electorate balks initiative and limits the choice of the people to candidates who have first won the approval of certain self-established coteries of citizens, is shown by the magnitude of the vain efforts of Hearst. He attempted to win the mayoralty without permission of the Democrats, the Republicans, or the organized reformers. He had newspapers in three languages, reaching an enormous clientèle. He built up an elaborate machine and astounded his rivals by the size of the crowds he drew to his mass meetings, for he tapped the enthusiasm of the radical element and the hope of the discontented. Never has a man been so elaborately and powerfully equipped for this fray. Yet he was twice defeated by Tammany Hall, which met him not with arguments, but by a more thorough canvass. Thorough canvassing wins elections, for the simple human reason that an argument personally delivered face to face is more compelling than a better argument shouted in the dim distance. Any thorough canvass of the voters was utterly impossible for Hearst's impromptu organization, or indeed for any organization save Tammany Hall itself, with its countless expert vote-getters to whom this work means bread and butter. The larger the electorate, the greater the advantage of a disciplined political army and the greater the advantage of an organization like Tammany Hall, which does not scruple to pay its soldiers out of the city treasury.

COMMISSION GOVERNMENT IN LARGE CITIES

Several large cities, for example, Pittsburg, Baltimore, Cincinnati, and Buffalo, are discussing the adoption of the Galveston commission form of government. New York City shows what the results would be, for its board of estimate is very similar to a commission. Applied to large cities, the commission plan would result in a short interesting ballot, but the Second Limitation of Democracy — wieldy districts — would be exceeded, and political machines would to some extent continue to share in the control of the government.

CHICAGO

Chicago has a mayor, many minor elective officers, and a board of aldermen elected singly from wards. The ballot is very long and mostly uninteresting, and the districts of most of the officers are unwieldy. The aldermen, contrary to general American custom, have large powers, and this has made possible an interesting development in local politics. Some years ago the Municipal Voters' League, consisting essentially of a half-dozen men and some money, started to improve what then was a notoriously corrupt board of aldermen. By concentrating their efforts on this body they made it artificially conspicuous, until the name of the alderman stood out rather prominently on the long ballot before the average voter, instead of being lost in the shuffle as before. This considerably negatived the peril of the long ballot so far as the office of alderman was concerned; and as the office played a large part in determining interesting policies and the district was wieldy, the effect of full conformity to our Two Limitations was obtained. The Municipal Voters' League did not nominate candidates, but confined its efforts to maintaining the well-aimed searchlight which prevented the aldermen from getting lost in the shadowy jungle of the huge Chicago ballot.

Thereupon democracy began to reveal itself, incidentally demonstrating that when the people get what they want, what they want proves to be better government than the politicians usually care to give them. Chicago began to see the spectacle of independent candidates for the board of aldermen appearing in various wards and winning. These independent candidates could muster a few friends, improvise a private electioneering organization competent to cover the little district, get credit before the people for superior merit (thanks to the illumination provided by the Voters' League), and gather in the votes. When there was no independent nomination, the fear that there might be one if the party nominations were not satisfactory was a well-founded fear and helped to put the parties on their good behavior. Moreover, if one party nominated a better candidate for alderman than the other party, it gained votes, whereas in the old days of gloom nobody would have noticed. The wieldiness of the district prevented the parties from establishing a defiant monopoly by combination; for both parties to make bad nominations was to invite an independent nomination that could defeat them both. (Note that there was no such danger in the case of offices elected at large from the "unwieldy" city!)

Year after year the board of aldermen in this environment showed steady improvement. The "gray wolves," who had been an apparently unassailable majority in the board, dropped out and stayed out and were replaced by men who, for instance, could be safely trusted to represent the people in traction matters. "Dropped out and stayed out"

FITS AND MISFITS

— that's the significant thing! Usually when reformers, seizing the government temporarily from the politicians, clean up a board of aldermen, they do it all at once. Then they see their work all undone at the next election, when their unnatural spasm of volunteer effort, which for a moment had overbalanced the paid efforts of the opposing professionals, relapses to the normal. But here is a board of aldermen that gets clean and stays so, as Galveston did, for example; and not through the widespread political organization of the people, but through providing an environment wherein the people, without organizing and thereby delegating discretion to a few, could deal directly with their servants. Chicago, so far as the aldermen are concerned, has a democratic government, and the benefits of democracy, of which better government is one, will continue to accrue so long as the artificial light is kept lighted. If Chicago could obtain a charter giving to the board of aldermen the right to appoint and control all other city officials, a short interesting ballot would replace the long stupid one and the Municipal Voters' League would find its faithful lamp made needless by a flood of natural sunlight.

The success of the Municipal Voters' League in Chicago has changed the direction of reform efforts in cities all over the country, and the old idea of forming new parties to fight for civic improvement has, in consequence, been largely abandoned. Imitations of the Municipal Voters' League in other places have often had indifferent success along the lines of the Chicago campaign. They can usually point to important achievements in other fields, but none of these voters' leagues, I think, can say honestly that they have brought about permanent reform in the city council. Their difficulty lies in the fact that the legislative bodies in most American cities are unimportant in their powers and unduly large in their membership. Often they are divided into two houses, on the well-disproved theory that if you make action of any kind awkward, the grafters will get tired of trying to put through their game. Membership in these councils is no honor, because it involves so small a share of the power. The members do not play a "large part in determining interesting policies," as in Chicago. So when the reformer in Philadelphia rushes into the newspaper offices with an accusation against Alderman Dennis, the editor, instead of giving it front-page headlines as would his Chicago confrère, shakes his head in a bored fashion, tucks the item away on a back page, and neglects to follow it up. He knows that the people will not get stirred up about so insignificant and obscure a public official — that they will not read any story of municipal scandal unless it touches some conspicuous personage, such as the mayor. A voters' league can compensate somewhat for the difficulties of invisibility by turning on the light; but to illumine a thing will not necessarily make the people stare; the thing must be interesting in itself. Except in cities where aldermen are individually powerful, the Voters' League recipe for putting the people in control of politics will not work.

THE BRITISH CITIES

The city governments of England and Scotland are the admiration of the world. They are intelligent, progressive, and economical. Ward politicians and reformers are both conspicuous by their absence. Yet to a political grafter of our country the opportunities would seem ideal. The British municipality is run by the council, acting through committees. There is considerable antiquated and outgrown red-tape, and the property interests in the House of Lords often interfere unreasonably with city progress. In some cities the municipal operation of public utilities — gas works, street cars, etc. — is so extended that one tenth of the laboring population is on the city pay-rolls, with none of the civil-service-examination restrictions that we should think vital in such a situation, to check "patronage." The development of wholesale organized corruption would seem to be inevitable in such an environment. Its absence is not to be explained by any superior civic spirit in the British public, for before the cities were organized under the present act relating to municipal corporations, corruption in their governments was widespread and quite equal in flagrancy to anything we have ever had in the United States. The explanation is seen when you ride down to business on the tramway on a morning following a meeting of the city council. The doings of the council are spread out in detail in the morning paper, the editorials review the proceedings, the people are chatting on the subject, each citizen knows what the councilmen from his ward did, and criticism is pointed and severe.

Everybody in town seems dissatisfied and the councilmen will know it. This is a phenomenon that also reveals itself in Des Moines and other cities in our country under the commission plan, and it sometimes gives to a casual observer the impression that the plan of government is anything but satisfactory to the people. But this criticism, on closer study, is found to be over matters an American would usually regard as trifles — matters which he never debates because so many larger affairs usually need fixing first. They are matters which in typical American towns are never looked into by the people at all. I have seen a city council in England bitterly denounced in an editorial because it had made an architect stick unreasonably close to specifications!

The existence of this ready and bitter criticism is not a sign of disease, but a sign of health.

The council dares not differ with public opinion. The lash is always busy. The members must explain themselves at every turn. The people not only have the right to oversee the work of their representatives, but they actually are on deck overseeing it. A British council would face a hurricane of public wrath if it did some things which an American city council could do with impunity. That difference is sufficient to account for the relative superiority of the British municipality. How was it brought about? By some great stirring up of the conscience of the people? Are the British citizens, by reason of being conscious taxpayers or for some other cause, more alert on civic matters than our people are? No. Remember that simile in the first chapter — the stream and the water-mill? The British water-mill works so nicely, not because the stream is stronger, but because the mill turns more easily, its gears being properly adjusted to the energy available.

The mechanism by which the British voter controls his city government is a ballot about the size of a post-card. It elects the member of council from his ward. There are two names, or three, on it; the voter selects one. To make up his mind on that simple choice is the whole work of the voter in the campaign and on election day. The chance of his selecting the candidate who really best represents his wishes is excellent — certainly much better than that of an American voter who is trying to make wise selections for thirty offices at one time! The British council chooses

FITS AND MISFITS

the aldermen (who sit in the council), the mayor, whose duties are mostly ornamental, and all other city officers. The councilmen simply dictate policies for paid superintendents to carry out. They do not themselves receive salaries and they give only their spare time to the city. The service does not mean the abandonment of private careers. The wards are small, and candidates can easily get in personal touch with every voter. The office is a visible and debatable office, since it has "a large part in determining interesting policies," and this fact leads to fierce campaign discussions. No candidate could hope for success if he did not permit questions to be publicly addressed to him at the conclusion of his speeches, and this "heckling" does much to provide a basis for clear opinions among the voters.

The phenomenon of political peace when things are going right is also noticeable here, for about one third of the time there is "no contest," which means either that at the expiration of his term no one cares to try to prevent the incumbent from remaining in office for another three years, or that only one candidate has asked to have his name printed on the official ballot. Councilmen who do well for one or more terms and are ready to serve again, are so sure to be reëlected that it is useless for new candidates to come forward. Often council members serve for decades.

This is good government, and it results from having a form of government which the people readily control. The British city is a democracy. The Two Limitations are respected:—

1. The office is visible.
2. The district is wieldy.

THE GOVERNMENT OF COUNTIES

The application of the Limitations to county government brings us face to face with a new difficulty: *all* the offices are practically undebatable. There may be a division of opinion as to which candidate ought to have the place and its salary, but that is not a subject of sufficient import to make the people take note of the matter and study it carefully enough to develop clear opinions. To county positions men can be, and frequently are, elected whom the people would not think of choosing if the facts were clearly and prominently brought to their attention. Men who have given good service are displaced without justice or recognition, and others whose service has been inferior are retained. There is little to encourage good behavior in office, and inefficiency is common.

All this holds true to a larger extent in big counties than in little ones. A small, compact, rural county partakes largely of village characteristics, and under these circumstances it will be found that not only is county politics a lively scramble for jobs, but the people are on hand to control it according to their own liking. When the people know each other and do not have to be educated to an acquaintance with the relative merits of the candidates, the long uninteresting ballot does not matter. Large counties and counties that include cities, on the other hand, are, and always will be, neglected by the people — a condition that is undemocratic as well as dangerous.

Concentrating the power of the county, consolidating the little offices, or creating a compact and powerful board of county supervisors to appoint the rest of the officers, is the easiest way to approach to conformity with the Two Limitations. In many counties where the people now pay no attention to the county government this treatment would be sufficient to throw the officialdom up into the limelight, where the people would see and criticise and control it. The biggest counties, however, would not respond. All the powers of the county, even if concentrated in the hands of a single official, are not enough to cause a big electorate to bestir itself to select the best man. The absence of anything truly political or policy-determining in the office would make it invisible, and the people would fail to control.

I believe that we shall ultimately find our way out of the county problem, not by inventing a short-ballot county with a responsible chief executive, but by gradually abolishing the county as an electoral unit. Any work performed on a small scale is usually relatively inefficient, and many county functions, such as the care of the insane and the poor, can be better administered on a large scale by the state. The slipshod methods of the typical county clerk cannot be tolerated forever, and the desirability of uniform methods throughout the state will bring these officers under central responsible control. Sheriffs may be replaced by officers of a state police enforcing the state laws; we cannot always tolerate the local nullification of statutes by leaving them to be enforced by independent, and therefore insubordinate, local elective officers. The constant speeding up of our means of communication is making our states steadily smaller, and changes of this sort are becoming easier as well as more desirable. Another way to get rid of at least part of this county problem is to extend the plan used, for instance, in Port Huron, Michigan, where the city officials appoint the local delegation to the board of supervisors.

To politicians who play their little hide-and-seek games in the county underbrush, such a mowing down may seem a catastrophe. The people, in shop and factory and field, will never miss the county or regret its passing.

JUDICIAL OFFICERS

The question whether judges should be elected or appointed is not to be determined by your opinion or mine as to whether such positions are properly political. It should be settled by the answer to the question, "Do the people want to select their judges?" That answer is not to be obtained by a referendum. The opinion of the theorizing voter is often a rather hazy thing. The answer is obtained by asking, "If the judicial elections were on separate days from other elections, would the bulk of the people study the relative merits of the candidates and go to the polls and make the selection? Or would the judicial election be ignored by all save a minority of the people?" I believe that outside of village justices the people would usually ignore the judges and allow bosses to put into office any reasonably respectable candidate. Except in some picturesque emergency, the office does not interest the people enough to make them come out and be counted.

The proponents of an appointive judiciary point to actual results. They can show that New Jersey, with its appointed judges, has a higher and abler class of men on the bench than New York, where judicial nominations are commonly said to be purchasable from Tammany for one hundred and fifty thousand dollars apiece. The Federal judiciary is considered by lawyers to be superior in honesty and ability to the elected judiciary of most of the states, despite the modesty of the Federal salaries.

But there is wide complaint that the appointed judges are habitually reactionary and lag behind the spirit of the times. Things which seemed just yesterday are counted unjust to-day. So much of our law is judge-made that a demand that the bench shall reflect the temper of the people so far as it can without stretching the statutes, is reasonable. That, however, does not prove that popular election will accomplish it. Making judges elective is not enough to make the people really choose the judges, and wherever experience establishes it as a fact that the populace does not take an active normal interest in the dull debates between the supporters of rival judiciary candidates, there is no choice but to make the judges appointive. To leave the selection to an uninterested, and hence unobserving, people is to leave it unguarded. It will then remain immune from spoliation only so long as the corrupt men among the people overlook the opportunity.

The right road to a judiciary that will be satisfactory to everybody is to improve the legislatures. Legislatures that are more accurately representative than those of to-day will make laws that will less often oblige the judges to hand down unpopular decisions. A reduction in the number of occasions for complaint will ultimately, I think, take judiciary positions far away from politics and popular agitation.

STATE LEGISLATURES

State legislatures play a large part in deciding interesting policies, but state legislators individually play a very small part in deciding them. Great as is the power of the whole legislature, it is successfully subdivided to extinction among an unduly large number of members. The best brains of the state are not in the legislatures, and will not go there when they can. The governorship will attract the ablest men at great personal sacrifice, but the offer of a seat among the law-makers will not for a moment tempt them from their private careers. The legislatures are full of beardless lawyers to whom the salary, small as it is, is important while their private practice is getting started. To be a legislator is not the ultimate goal of their careers, but a pot-boiler of the early stages. Even the public leaders, fighting for popular principles, often prefer not to accept a legislative nomination, but to do their work in getting desirable laws enacted, from outside. Often a party committee will search to find a desirable man who is willing to accept the post; for it is no light thing for a man of ability to halt his private progress to take a public office in which there is so little private satisfaction or public recognition. Men will take an office in which they anticipate no glory, if they can really feel that what they do there serves their fellow men, but they find few such opportunities in a state legislature. The power is so slight! An assemblyman in New York, for example, is only one one hundred and fiftieth of one half of a legislature that is hedged in by elaborate constitutional restrictions and subject to the governor's veto. No one can blame him if he returns to his constituents with none of his purposes achieved. His powers are negative rather than positive, and hence he cannot win public attention because his position is uninteresting.

I once asked several hundred voters in Brooklyn on the day after election day if they knew the names of the candidates for assemblymen in their district, — the most independent district in the state, — and of those who were willing to reveal their ignorance, only sixteen per cent could give the names of both candidates. This was in a year when wide agitation had brought the legislature into unusual prominence. I am certain that most of the voters had opinions to express on the issue of "Direct Nominations," for which Governor Hughes had been fighting; but in voting without knowing the attitude of their own assemblymen on the subject they were certainly not expressing these opinions. The people in many cases must have been voting against the thing they wanted to support. The legislature, I repeat, determines interesting policies, but the individual legislator does not play a large part therein and the First Limitation of Democracy is exceeded; the office is not visible.

Now, legislators cannot be made appointive. To leave them elective and diminish their importance by providing other ways of lawmaking, such as the initiative and referendum, is to divert what little light now shines upon them, and, if the logic of the preceding chapters is accurate, such movements are in the wrong direction, useful though they may be as expedients to meet present conditions.

A better diagnosis of the failure of legislatures to satisfy public opinion may be based on that symptom in Brooklyn, where the people were thinking one way and voting another. "Delegated government," or representative government, we are being told, has

FITS AND MISFITS 105

broken down in this country, and we are going to progress to better things by means of democratic substitutes of which the chief is the referendum. This is much the same reasoning as that which induces New York to take the franchise-granting power away from the New York City aldermen and give it to the board of estimate, because the aldermen have been untrustworthy and the board of estimate is more honest. As an expedient — good enough. But if the aldermen cannot be trusted with franchises, can they be trusted with anything else? Should they not either be made trustworthy or be abolished?

In the case of legislative representatives, tucking them off in a hole and doing our business some other way may be expedient for the time, but it is not an end of the problem unless we are intending to do all our business the new way. And we are not. We shall always need legislatures and shall always have to make use of them to execute the details of our commands in the spirit of our mandate. The real answer to present legislative disobedience to the desires of the people is to make legislators responsive to popular control, and that is a mere matter of adjusting the machinery of control so that when the people have a wish, it will be to the interest of legislators to obey and obey quickly.

At present the legislator has no motive to inquire, "Will my vote on this measure please my constituents?" for his constituents will not even notice how he voted, although they may be interested in the measure. How different is the governor's position! His decision will set a million voters talking, and his strength with the people fluctuates every time he signs or vetoes a bill which interests them. The voters constantly stand at the governor's elbow, overseeing his work, prodding, suggesting, criticising, applauding, jeering or demanding — and, on election day, voting! And thereby depends much that is important to the governor — not merely continuance in office, but vindication, honor, satisfaction, a political career, all that is involved in conspicuous success. The rewards for serving the people to their satisfaction are sweet and the penalties for bad service are bitter — for a governor.

If we could get our legislative representatives into a similar environment we should have less to complain of. Theoretically the

FITS AND MISFITS 107

legislator who votes the unpopular way gets punished, as the governor does. Practically he does not suffer at all. The typical voter cheers on the progress of a popular measure at the Capitol, damns the governor who opposes it, but has nothing to say, even on the ballot on election day, in derogation of the obscure legislative representatives who also oppose it. This comparative immunity from popular disapproval makes defiance of popular desires easy for our legislatures, and constitutes an unlighted environment so unhealthy as to account fully for a "failure of representative government." Of course it fails! Representative government in our states has nowhere been tried as yet under conditions which give it a ghost of a show for success!

Now suppose we go in imagination to the opposite extreme with our legislatures and increase the importance of the individual members until they tower up into public view as governors do and become correspondingly sensitive! That would mean reducing the total number of members to, say, thirty, in a large state like New York or ten in a little state like Maryland. It would mean also an end of the tangle-foot double-chamber plan, and the members would sit as a single body, as a constitutional convention does, with the ability to act swiftly for good or ill. Remove also the elaborate limitations of the state constitution, leaving only the simplest outlines so that the courts would not have to be incessantly throwing statutes into the waste-basket. *Then* to be a legislator would be a big honor! The people would be up on tiptoe to see that the candidates suited them. Newspapers, instead of editorially condemning the corruption of the legislature in the broad general terms which now hit nobody, would be talking about Representative Smith's folly in trying to defeat this bill and Representative Jones's continued stupidity in urging that one; while the mere suspicion of dishonorable conduct by any representative would start mass meetings all over his district.

Of course, the reduction in size of the legislature must take into account the necessity of keeping the districts wieldy. How much too far we should be going in cutting the New York State legislature to thirty members and one house, I do not know. But we ought to go far enough in that direction to attract to each member such a glare of natural public scrutiny as will make it inevitable that the people will see what they are doing on election day. To go less far is unsafe, as experience shows us. To go too far is not so perilous as it looks. Government in the light is safer than government in the dark. And as only in the light can the people see to control their government, government in the light alone is popular government.

THE STATE ADMINISTRATION

In New York State forty-nine officials, with annual salaries of four thousand to fifteen thousand dollars, are subject to the appointment of the governor. There are in addition (besides the lieutenant-governor) five minor elective officers, with salaries of five thousand dollars a year — namely, secretary of state, comptroller, state treasurer, attorney-general, and state engineer-and-surveyor. Several of the appointed officers are more important than all these elective ones put together. To make them all appointive would not add ten per cent to the governor's power. When the legislature in 1908 passed the bill which created the appointive Public Service Commissions, it gave to the governor a greater addition of power than he would acquire if he were allowed to appoint the rest of the present state ticket.

In other states there is wide variation. New Jersey has no elective administrative offices except the governor. There is not even an elective lieutenant-governor. Ohio, Illinois, California, South Dakota, Oklahoma, and most of the remaining states go to the other extreme and make the voters choose a great mass of petty state officers, such as the state printer, trustees of the state university, dairy and food commissioner, etc. The choice of which officers to elect and which to appoint seems to have been entirely capricious.

In all cases these officers are invisible. If by a printer's error one of these little officers should be omitted from the ballot, the voters, if not notified, would vote the ticket and be none the wiser. If the Democratic nominee for state engineer in New York were by a printer's error slipped into the Republican column, he would be elected with the Republicans, unless the voters could be warned; and there would be a pretty legal tangle to determine whether the multitude who voted a straight ticket were supposed to know what they were doing or not.

FITS AND MISFITS

A conscientious voter trying to accomplish the unnatural and uninteresting task of finding out which of the various candidates for state treasurer was best fitted for his job, would be unable to discover enough information about them in the newspapers to justify the formation of an opinion. Of general public criticism and counter-criticism there is none. A candidate can get elected without making a single public speech to plead that he is superior in qualifications for the office.

The people, voting as they think best when they know what they think, and blindly endorsing the party machine in the case of the obscure offices, are doing wisely. Voting a straight ticket is at least better than voting at random, for a party machine is somewhat responsible and somewhat desirous of making a good showing. But the fact that the great body of voters will support any respectable figure whom the party machine decides to nominate, leaves to the machine complete discretion in the matter. Accordingly at state conventions the choice of candidate for governor is almost solely dependent upon what the people will think, and the choice of minor offices is almost solely dependent upon what a few politicians think. The whole matter is settled by a dozen men in the conventions of the two principal parties; and while there may be some doubt as to which of the two party groups will win, — a matter in which the merit of these minor nominations plays only an insignificant part, — there is no doubt that these two groups hold between them a perfect and unassailable monopoly. There is no possibility of a successful independent ungrouped candidacy for a minor state office, to act as a check upon the exercise of the bosses' discretion. Under either the convention system or any other nominating plan, the absence of the people from the whole discussion leaves control in the hands of the few who are interested enough to take a hand in the matter.

The plan of having the people select these minor state officials has been attempted and has failed. The experiment has been thoroughly made and the plan has not worked. That fact is sufficient reason for its abandonment. The contrary idea of appealing to the people, by exhortation and prayer, to take an interest in an uninteresting thing, is futile. Human nature may alter in that direction some day, but we cannot wait to see!

LIEUTENANT-GOVERNORS

Our natural sentiment favors the selection by the people of the man who takes the governor's place in case of death. The average American thinks of the post as one which the people should fill by election. I fancy that most citizens in New Jersey, where the successor of the governor is not elective, would quietly applaud a movement in a constitutional convention to provide for an elective lieutenant-governor like other states.

This, for most constitution-writers, real or imaginary, would settle the matter. But you and I are cranks and we inquire further. The plan of requiring the people to choose lieutenant-governors has been tried. Has it worked? Do the people select their lieutenant-governors?

I think not. Can you, as a sample citizen, give offhand the full name of the lieutenant-governor of your state? Did you have anything to say about his selection before the matter was settled for you by the powers of the party machine? Did the question agitate the public mind as the selection of the gubernatorial candidate did? Did the public opinion which named the eligible list for the governorship name also an eligible list for lieutenant-governor?

Is n't it true that often the people of your state have compelled the nomination of a champion of certain policies and ideals for the governorship, and have indolently permitted the party to name on the same ticket for lieutenant-governor some party hack whose policies and ideals were just the opposite? How often have the people elected a lieutenant-governor whom they would not have approved of for a moment if during the campaign a serious illness of his superior had brought him out of his obscurity into "that fierce light which beats upon the throne"?

The election of a man whom the people would not favor if they knew him, demonstrates that the voters have not functioned at the polls as the constitutional convention wanted them to. The intentions of those who devised the plan were good, but, when tried, the plan did not result in popular control. There is no appealing from the test of practice to reason and theory. The office is not visible.

In offering a theory to explain the results of

the test of practice, I am adding only non-essential comment for the comfort of the stubborn reasoner who says, "Drat it — the idea ought to work anyhow!" No. It ought not to be expected to work in view of the fact that one vital factor in the plan is a mass of human beings who, as at present constituted, do not interest themselves in uninteresting things except under compulsion. And the people are too big to be spanked.

Should we really be disturbed if the death of a lieutenant-governor at the beginning of his term left the succession to an official whom the people did not elect?

CHIEF EXECUTIVES

In the case of governor or president, the office is visible. The district, except in the smallest states, is not wieldy. Our relative success as a people in controlling those offices demonstrates that visibility is more vital than wieldiness of district. Even though we must use the politicians' own machinery to establish a hopeful nomination, independent campaigns for the governorship or presidency being almost impossibly difficult, we have often specified the very man who should be chosen and almost always are obeyed in our requirements as to the type of man who shall be selected. Nevertheless, in very many cases the conditions are far from being satisfactory, and the people find that they are sharing the control of these officers with sinister self-established coteries of political specialists.

Yet the very men who express horror at the short-ballot doctrine, fearing that it leads toward autocracy and kings, would take most offense at any proposal to dispense with our powerful chief executive. But if the people are to have unthreatened and complete control over all sources of governmental authority, some way must be found by which the people can dispense with the help of the professional politician, when undertaking to hire a good man for governor.

There are various ways of managing it, and I grant you in advance we shall never adopt any of them. One way — a bad one — is to district the state and let electors be chosen from each district, later to meet, deliberate and select a chief magistrate. In the case of the President and Vice-President of the United States, this was done. But the popular mind hurdled over the barriers and insisted on dis-

FITS AND MISFITS 117

cussing ultimate consequences, until the delegates to the Electoral College became automata and the whole device dwindled in importance until it has become a mere vermiform appendix of our political system.

Another solution — a good one — is to let the legislature — our improved limelighted legislature — elect the governor and control him, somewhat as Parliament performs executive functions through its prime minister, or as the board of directors chooses the chief executive of a corporation.

But our chief executives appeal to the popular imagination so much that no such proposal would ever obtain a fair hearing on its merits. I believe, however, we shall arrive at our goal of popular control by a new route. The change of the rest of our system to a workable popular basis will so weaken the present party machines, by destroying most of the strategic advantages which they now enjoy, that they will be easy to cope with. The change will also clear the way for new parties representing fresh ideas and ideals, and will give them a chance to live and grow to an effective size, whereas now they die a-borning. The way will be cleared also for new kinds of parties, and in new kind of parties, based unshakably on genuine principles, we must seek the solution of the remaining political awkwardnesses of the people.

CHAPTER VIII

RAMSHACKLE GOVERNMENT

BARE compliance with the foregoing Limitations of Democracy may not be enough to carry us all the way to popular control. Respect for these Limitations puts the people in the driver's seat where they can readily reach and operate all the controlling levers. But suppose the governmental organization be like one of those first unreliable coffee-mill cars of the earliest days of the automobile industry, so loose and weakly jointed that it is incapable of obeying the people effectively, no matter how hard they work the levers? Such a government is the most supinely disobedient government imaginable and a government that is likely to disobey so continually cannot be called a democracy!

The favorite and cleverest American method of balking the people in this fashion is based on our ancient superstitious belief in "checks and balances" and the "separation of powers." An imaginary instance helps to keep us clear of old fallacies, so let us do some supposing. Suppose the people of this country are to send to Europe a group of popular representatives to conduct certain important negotiations and labors. Having elected the right men by adherence to the Two Limitations we have been discussing, do we then proceed to allow them to sit as one body, hire their own expert help, execute their own decisions and take responsibility for securing for us the results we want? Oh no! Forsooth we must pick out one member from that delegation, isolate him and give him power to undo the work of all the others with a veto! Then we must divide the remainder into two houses so as to multiply chances for disagreement and "make it hard for a bad measure to get through." Then as there will be certain clerks and financial officials needed to handle details of this work, we will ourselves pick out other members of the delegation, call them clerk, treasurer, etc., and give them certain independent powers of oversight and interference. And when we shipped this complicated ramshackle organization to Europe, we should expect it to handle its work efficiently without deadlocks, hold-ups, delays, or quarrels!

Why, it is organized for inefficiency! If that

treasurer, for example, has a pet idea of his own, he has power to hold up the rest of the delegation on various pretexts until he has compelled them to acquiesce. Each house, and each officer, being independent of the rest, has opportunities to trade and log-roll, and being protected in the right, cannot be squelched by the majority. If the clerk furnished poor co-operation with the rest of the delegation, they would have to make the best of it, for they are not his masters. If the whole result of such organization were chaos and deadlock, the rational cure would be to bring all the members of the delegation together as one body with a single vote apiece, let them thresh out their differences in discussion and then settle the matter by the simple process of taking votes and ordering the carrying out of the decisions by servants of their own who would have no authority to "talk back." And that would bring you back to the original natural plan of vesting all the power in a single body!

The British city elects perhaps twenty men who sit in a single-chambered council with no other elective city officials to interfere with them, and the British city gets results.

The American city elects twenty men who

sit on several separate statutory pedestals, called "Council," "Mayor," "Board of Works," "Tax Commission," "Comptroller," etc., each having power to slap the face of the others, and when the people fail to secure obedience to their will, they must burrow through a labyrinth of detail to find out who is responsible for the hold-up. The plan so multiplies the blocking power of honest disagreements that the government, like an automobile with a separate motor at every wheel, is almost incapable of that orderly harmony which is necessary for efficient low-frictioned action.

A city so organized might have, and often does have, a Short Ballot with no obscure offices, and wieldy districts. But without a reasonable "Unification of Powers" to enable it to obey the people, it may simply quiver under the jerked levers and helplessly fail to move as directed.

To be sure, if we have elected the right men they may waive their differences, may not take advantage of opportunities to block and check when they are in the minority, may not use the chances to betray the people without getting spotted. But in a complete democracy the mechanism must be designed so that harmony of action can be compelled—not merely urged.

"Unification of Powers" makes it possible to secure the necessary clear public location of responsibility. In our city plan of government, for instance, responsibility is obscured. When something goes wrong, the people blame the mayor, the mayor tells them to blame the council, the council tells them to blame the board of works, and the board of works blames the mayor, thus sending the people around a circle without giving them any satisfaction. Each officer in the circle may really have a valid excuse and might conceivably ask and secure reëlection year after year while the people are vainly trying to enforce their will. Making an officer's responsibility invisible is as undesirable as making the officer himself invisible. The practical solution sometimes is for the people to secure unity of control by allowing a boss to put in power puppets who will yield to his dictation, and then hold the boss morally responsible!

There is obviously a loss in the ability of the people to hold an official accountable if they themselves choose his subordinates. The stockholders of a corporation who choose not merely the directors but also the business manager would not thus gain additional control over the business, but would lose. In choosing the manager they are diminishing the power of their other servants, the directors, and are furnishing the latter with an opportunity to say "It's not *our* fault" when things go wrong. Likewise, in our cities which elect a council and mayor, the people have no more "power" than the people of a city which elects only a council. In the latter case the people's council is more powerful,—that's all, and the *control* by the people, which is the real thing we are after, is the more complete in the simpler plan.

The innate inefficiency of even the simplest instance of separated powers is seen in cities governed by mayor and council where the mayor's selections of his executive helpers require confirmation by the council, while the council makes ordinances and appropriations and levies the taxes. Generally, an exchange of functions ensues. The members of the council, not being held responsible for the conduct of the administrative departments, either legally or in the popular mind, proceed to interfere recklessly with departmental appointments, refusing to coöperate with the mayor until their friends have been given lucrative positions. As the mayor, not they, will be responsible for the work of these appointees, they need not worry about the capacity of these men to earn their salaries. In exchange, the council permits the mayor to plan and initiate most of the municipal legislation and draw up the budget. As the council, not he, will be responsible for the bigness of the appropriations and the corresponding bigness of the tax levy, the mayor has small inducement to economize. Similar exchanges of power without exchange of responsibility are seen in the state and national governments whose powers are likewise divided, and the general interests of the community suffer.

Such conditions increase the friction in the government, increase the frictional resistance to popular demand, and make the government less obedient, less sensitive to the controlling levers. And thus the people find themselves balked and baffled, get discouraged, make fewer demands and make them more half-heartedly in a spirit of speculation as to whether this time the shaky ramshackle may not happen to respond. And in taking this attitude, as in everything else, the people are quite possibly right.— The trouble of getting an improvement or stopping a graft may in some circumstances actually be greater than the resulting advantage warrants. The civic inertia in many an American city has vanished immediately upon the adoption of the sensitive Commission Plan of Government. "Our people seem to have been made over," says an experienced official and ex-mayor of Des Moines. "They are interested in municipal matters now and are willing to subscribe money and energy for city improvement with an unflagging enthusiasm we never saw before."

Another ingenious American way of balking the people, even when they find themselves at the controlling levers of a workable car, is to tie the steering wheel. State constitutional conventions, which assume legislative functions and crystallize their humanly defective foresight into rigid written documents, often do this. So do legislatures, which hand down to cities specifically enumerated and limited powers, and charters, which inflexibly regulate administration down to its details so that every improvement in efficiency calls for the passage of a special enabling act or amendment by remote and uncomprehending legislators. The idea of thus tying up the steering wheel and shortening its turning arc is to make it certain that the car will go straight ahead. "Straight ahead" may lead over bumps and stones and through deep, speed-slackening sand. Flexibility is essential to responsiveness and real control. The elective public servants, who constitute the people's steering wheel, are not servants at all if they are bound hand and foot by red-tape. Constitutions, unless made primitively short and simple or made of rubber by great ease of amendment as in Oklahoma, are often not guarantees of liberty, but rather denials of popular control. Often we see roundabout evasion of a state constitution frankly managed and justified as a triumph of the popular will over an obstacle!

Simple and thoroughly unified governments that can do things, simple state constitutions, municipal home rule, and county home rule on the new California plan which allows each county to devise and run its own government — all these and more things, too, are among the requirements that demand consideration in building a democracy that will "democ."

Condensing the idea further — *the government must be strong and unhampered.* This is a Third Limitation of Democracy.

Weak, disjointed, ramshackle governments are more than ever undemocratic in these days of the great private corporations which in their wealth and resources loom over our feeble public organizations and make the latter look like infants policing giants. Considering how the people are contesting with private powers for the control of privilege and the natural sources of wealth, the demand for stronger governments, unhampered governments that *can* obey, becomes part of the unwritten modern bill of rights. You will find when you speak of governmental simplification to a politician, he will cry, "That's conferring too much power!" One of his cronies, that famous beast called "Privilege," will say the same, for Privilege dearly loves to race with a slow, wheezy machine that runs uncertainly and stops frequently for readjustments and repairs! But your champion of popular rights will not shiver a bit. The people will perhaps want to wait till they are surely in control. They have seen other untrusted forces controlling so much in the past that to increase the strength of the governments begets fear of misuse of the enlarged powers. So no doubt we shall have to be content with getting the Short Ballot first. When the people find in their hands all the instruments of control, they will no longer fear to have stripped away the hampering checks and balances and legal interferences of the present régime.

CHAPTER IX

PARTIES AND WHY THEY CANNOT BE RESPONSIBLE

WHEN the clumsiness and complexity of politics leave the bulk of the people staring helplessly into its shadowy jungle, those few volunteers who leave other occupations and go in and master the ramifications and practical details of it are called "politicians." Or, to reverse the definition, a politician is a citizen who knows what he is doing on election day.

When a political system is incomplete, stretching only part way toward the up-reaching people who are supposed to operate it, the necessary improvised informal volunteer machinery that fills the gap is called a "political machine."

When a considerable number of the people come to believe in a certain state policy, in distinction to others of the people who disbelieve in it, the groups are called "parties."

A party to be effective needs some sort of

organization to bring about unity of action among its members — hence the formation of party machinery and of party machines. The machines, in operating a governmental mechanism so complicated that their actions are not subject to adequate review by the rank and file of the party, acquire the opportunity to use unchecked discretion in the name of the party and become more powerful than the party. Originally intended to be only the obedient steering-engine of the ship, responsive to the touch of the wheel on the captain's bridge, the party machine has become conscious of its power to direct the ship and has done so, thereby acquiring virtual command. The object of a party is the installation of a principle in the government. The object of a party machine is continuance in power. The party and the machine are two very different things.

The Republican party, for example, was at the time of its foundation a genuine party founded for a specific purpose. This object was successfully accomplished, and after a few years when all danger that the nation might undo the work was safely past, all reason for the further existence of the Republican party had vanished. From that time on, the Republican party was not a true party at all, inasmuch as its members were not a group of voters bonded together to establish a principle. New questions arose, upon which Republicans were not all agreed; the party lines no longer followed certain planes of natural cleavage of opinion, and the "party" became an artificial and purposeless union of more or less uncongenial voters. But the powerful party machines were still existent and had no thought of consenting to be sent to the scrap-heap. Thenceforward the Republican party was only a machine, plus an enrollment of more or less willing, habit-driven voters. A Republican victory after the war meant the triumph of no particular principle, but only the success of a machine in grasping power. From a position of power in the machine the high-minded men who founded it for a purpose were soon displaced in favor of men who were more effective machinists. So far as possible new principles were suppressed lest they divide the party's following. When issues became too important to be either ignored or straddled, the Republican party would take one side, the Democratic party the other. All good Republicans were expected to adjust their ideas accordingly and become high protectionists and gold-standard advocates, while all good Democrats were expected to change or ignore their individual convictions rather than wrench themselves away from their dear party. Party loyalty was enthusiastically fostered by the machine-workers, and the mugwump who varied from one party to another according to the policies advanced was jeered and scorned.

There is nothing much funnier in our American politics than the wild pawing-in-the-air of campaign orators who attempt to treat the party as if it were a real party representing some common idea of its members — the scurrying after "issues," the attempt to make every good thing that has happened appear to be of Republican creation and every bad thing Democratic — or *vice versa!* What uncanny coincidence of opinion, that the people who agree on national policies should also be of one mind in the entirely separate discussion of state policies, county policies, and city policies! How vague the orator becomes when he apostrophizes those strangely agile principles of the party which can fit so many diverse situations!

Of course the thing is simply unbelievable.

Persistent arguing by reformers in our cities has convinced the people that national policies have no bearing upon city policies, and the fact that a man approves Republican national policies is no reason why he should approve what happen to be "Republican" city policies. But although we have been less often urged to recognize it, there is no natural unity between state and national parties either. We ought in theory to have one set of national parties battling on national policies, other sets of state parties dividing on state issues, sets of parties in each county, each city, each township. For on each of these political battle-fields the grouping of men according to their opinions will produce different combinations. To make the same company fight as a unit for so many different causes means inevitably that some of the soldiers will be on sides they do not really favor and thus public opinion is suppressed.

In fact, it is only logical to carry the idea further. When the coroner is made elective, it is to be presumed that there is opportunity there for a difference of opinion—that, for instance, the people are expected to divide on such issues as whether to elect a coroner who proposes to buy an automobile to answer calls quickly, or to elect his opponent who will save money and let the cases wait while he comes by street car. No issues concerning the coronership can possibly be allied to issues concerning the county clerkship, the sheriff's office, or the surrogate's or any other office. Accordingly, if parties are to consist of people who agree on a given policy, we must have separate parties for every office! Of course this is absolutely impracticable, but it serves to illustrate how utterly impossible it is for any such complicated system as ours, with its multiplicity of elective offices, to be, at all these points of contact with the people, responsive to their movements. Long ballots, so far from making the government sensitive to public opinion, actually balk and bewilder public opinion, making it certain that multitudes will ever be voting against their own desires.

Unable to operate so complicated a keyboard, the people have done the next best thing and have delegated their functions wholesale to the party machines. Average voters use their own judgment so far as they have light, and put responsibility for all the rest of the work upon the party. Few voters in large communities can name all the men they vote for on any election day. They vote for governors, mayors, and presidents in accordance with well-considered opinions, but for the "invisible" state treasurers, members of legislatures, county clerks, city solicitors, etc., they vote a straight ticket without even reading the names. It would do them small good if they did read the names, for the minor offices rarely have enough to do with interesting policies to furnish food for discussion, and in consequence the newspapers pay little attention to them. If the party label were unexpectedly omitted from the ballot, most voters would pore over the list of names helplessly, and would consider themselves clever if they could so much as recollect which of the minor candidates had been nominated by their party. There is no idea in the citizen's mind of comparing the candidates man for man, and selecting the best man in each case. He lacks the information on which to base an opinion, and in voting a straight ticket he expresses none, except to show that he considers the bosses in *his* party more reliable than the gang that runs the *other* party. Theoretically, if his party nominates a bad man for county clerk it will

PARTIES

suffer in due proportion by alienation of votes; but the absence of public scrutiny smashes the theory and the party can in fact nominate a bad man or a good man without causing serious fluctuation among its blind supporters. Of course if the vote is close enough to catch the five per cent or ten per cent of fluctuation that may result, a split ticket instead of the straight ticket will get elected. But as a rule the whole ticket will stand or fall as a unit.

This blind delegation of control to the party machine gives it a complete discretion which it is more than ready to use. Knowing that the public will accept any reasonably respectable figure nominated by the party, and will not respond to any efforts to win it with a superior quality of offerings for invisible offices, the party managers simply exclude the people's wish from further consideration. Whatever that wish may be, it won't be expressed in the voting, — so why cater to it? Accordingly, at the state convention for instance, assembling to nominate candidates for governor, lieutenant-governor, secretary of state, attorney-general, etc., a small group prepares a "slate." The bosslets come before this group intriguing, bargaining, threatening, bluffing, and pleading for a share of the pie of patronage. This coterie becomes the clearing house, a slate is prepared that balances up the conflicting claims as evenly as possible, resulting usually in division, regardless of the merit of candidates, on a geographical basis, and the slate is presented to the convention and accepted intact.

The bosslet who has wrested from the committee the right to name the attorney-general of the state naturally expects that the nominee after election will be duly grateful and will repay him out of the treasury of the state. The payment may be in the form of jobs that are easy enough to leave time for political activity, or in the form of "influence" that can be privately marketed to seekers of privilege. It is all very simple and very familiar, and it all has its root in the fact that the people have not been *se*lecting such officials but have only been *e*lecting them. The party machine has acquired and is exercising a power that properly should remain in the hands of the people.

Now to give a party machine the right to make a nomination is not giving it any power whatever if that nomination is to be adequately scrutinized, and if also there is chance for a competitor to enter the contest. A corrupt machine is powerless to do evil under such circumstances and is not in the least dangerous. But when scrutiny is wanting, the machine is left with unchecked discretion, and that is power — great power.

I can safely purchase apples from any merchant if I am allowed to subject the entire barrel to adequate examination. But if the merchants know I cannot do more than look at the top of the barrel, sooner or later some merchant will put bricks in the bottom and I shall be cheated. My natural recourse is to trade only at a shop where my experience has been satisfactory.

We patronize the party shop in this way when we acquire the habit of voting a ticket with a certain label. But there is this distinction: the apple shop remains in the same hands year after year; if the rival merchant wants to cheat me, he cannot easily acquire control of the store where I trade and thus get into a position where he can take advantage of my confidence.

But the political shop is constantly changing hands. The controlling spirits in it to-day are only a minority to-morrow. Rarely does a state now permit a party to be a "close corporation." The parties are governed, ultimately, by the rank and file — a topsy-turvy army in which the generals are elected by the captains and the captains by the privates. And the privates consist of anybody who wants to join. A political machine cannot resist contamination. Any man, honest or otherwise, may join it and must be welcomed. In many states the law specifically protects him in the privilege of enrolling and of sharing in the internal government of the party.

To place political power in such unguarded exposure is to make it certain that the power will sooner or later fall into the hands of corrupt men. The whole process is automatic and inevitable. The opportunity to cheat will attract the cheaters — and the cheaters must be welcomed. To say that the dominant political machine in every community is corrupt is no reflection on the community or even on the machine — it is only another way of saying that the dominant machine is the one that gets corrupted. The moment it acquires power, the grafters begin to join it. There is no advantage in corrupting a party that is in a hopeless minority.

PARTIES

The Prohibition party is probably as pure as the water it advocates. But let that party become dominant in any community and it will soon find its ranks filled with men who are there for plunder, the clergymen will find themselves outvoted in its conventions and committees, and its candidates will as likely as not be saloon-keepers. Certainly a party in which saloon-keepers and their sympathizers are freely permitted to enroll, may not always be a Prohibition party, if such enrollment means sharing in the control of party policies and nominations.

The Citizens' Union in New York City is another instance. At one time it became a large party with subsidiary organizations in every district and a huge enrollment. It outvoted the Republican party at one election, and fused with it and won the election the next time. It was organized on the idea of non-partisanship, and its founders sincerely disclaimed all intention of using patronage. Despite the fact that "no patronage" was the issue on which it acquired its power, the originators soon found that its ranks were full of Tammany men who had changed over to the winning side. The reformers found themselves shoulder to shoulder with men who had not taken the ideals of the Union seriously, who clamored for patronage and demanded that the officials whom they had elected allow them to sack the town exactly as Tammany had in the past. When the elected officials proved "ungrateful" and unwilling to create a permanent Citizens' Union machine and support it out of the city treasury, these helpers were bitterly aggrieved, and the Union was rent with internal warfare. The altruists won eventually, but only after a long fight in which the party's political strength was recklessly sacrificed to save the principle.

In Philadelphia the state law governing primary procedure makes entrance to a party quick and easy. The reformers organize a reform party and nominate reform candidates. Immediately the grafters enroll in the new party, and the next time the party makes nominations the reformers find themselves outvoted by their new and unwelcome associates and the reform party nominates grafters. Thereupon the true reformers hold an indignation meeting, adopt a new name, establish a new party, leaving the previous one to an early death — and the procedure is repeated.

There are two answers to the difficulty. One is to deprive the party of all power by subjecting its nominations to popular examination, under such circumstances that every improper nomination will be easily detected, and will result in the immediate offering of something more satisfactory by active or latent political competitors. Full obedience to the Limitations of Democracy would place the people in a political environment where they could at any moment dispense with unfaithful leadership and thus make cheating unprofitable.

But in a previous chapter I agreed that we were never likely to dispense with elected presidents and governors, the unwieldiness of whose districts will always leave some work for political machines. We must eventually adopt also another expedient — namely, build machines right side up, and make guarded leaders responsible for the party policies, leaving the people fancy-free to rally to the party of whichever leaders win their confidence.

CHAPTER X

"LEADERSHIP PARTIES"

THE government should be a democracy, but the party should be an autocracy. And, curiously enough, to make the parties autocratic will help to make the government a democracy. In no other way except by clumsy initiative and referendum devices can we separate the people into principle-united groups to be counted at elections so that their wishes can be accurately determined.

At present writing (1911) there is in the United States a strong insurgent progressive movement led by certain men in Congress, with a probable majority of the people in the country ready to follow their leadership. The Progressives are dissatisfied with both the old parties and suspicious of their managements. If no new party is formed, lack of organization and direction will leave the Progressives scattered, confused, and far less effective than their numbers entitle them to be. If a new party is formed on the traditional plan, the Progressives will promptly join it, but so will many others who are not true Progressives at all.

As soon as it becomes completely organized, the contamination starting among the rank and file will work upward, and if the prizes of power be sufficiently attractive to corrupt non-Progressive privilege-seekers, such men will work their way into control. The original leaders around whom the party rallied will be displaced by more conservative and "practical" men and in four years or less the Progressive party will have no principles on which all its members agree, the party vote will no longer represent a solid unit of opinion, and the real Progressives will be dismayed to see their name used as a mask for all sorts of movements which they do not approve of.

In trying to protect present-day parties against such invasions, the idealists face most unequal odds. They fight, unremunerated and thanklessly, for principle. They work as volunteers, and the work they do at caucuses and primaries and in "arousing the people" to the dangers, is at the expense of their efficiency in private work. It means sacrifice of self, family interests, pleasures, money, and commercial or professional progress. Accordingly their work must be limited in amount and sporadic. It cannot be incessant and thorough.

Against them are the self-seekers, to whom a principle seems wholly academic and amateurish. To them success *means* a livelihood and a career, whereas to the volunteers success *is at the cost of* livelihood and career. To the professional, intrigue, circumvention of ideals, and petty political details are a normal part of the day's work. The man with the fewest ideals has the fewest handicaps in the peanut politics incident to factional strife.

If the Progressives form a party of the old type therefore, this party will not long remain true to its ideals and the Progressives will soon be again without a rallying-point. Just as in New York State now certain Republican district conventions declare against the proposed Direct Nominations' law, while in adjoining districts other Republican conventions are favoring the measure, so the Progressive party would soon be a principle-dodging or divided machine plus a miscellaneous enrollment, instead of a great union of believers in certain principles.

The Progressives are in fact simply the fol-

"LEADERSHIP PARTIES" 147

lowers of certain conspicuous, well-known, and well-beloved leaders. Why not recognize the fact frankly and build on it?

Suppose a group of these leaders who have perfect mutual confidence form themselves into "The Progressive Committee." They agree that their membership in that committee shall be unassailable. They fill by appointment all vacancies in their own number that may occur by death or resignation. When congressional elections approach they meet and draw up the Progressive platform of the year, detailing those legislative proposals which they believe should be enacted by the next Congress. When this platform is published, the desire to win the support of Progressive voters will lead some candidates publicly to endorse the platform. Sometimes these candidates will be sincere, sometimes not. In some districts all candidates will endorse the platform; in other districts all the candidates will dodge it or oppose it. The Progressive Committee, after due examination of conditions and candidates in the various districts, issues its endorsement to one man in each (calling a new candidate into the field if necessary), saying to the people, "This man in your district has subscribed to the Progressive platform; we believe him sincere and capable; we hope you will elect him."

If the Progressive Committee did truly enjoy the confidence of the Progressive voters, this hoisting of the colors would rally the party effectively year after year.

True Progressives would be glad to find in the field a candidate who represented them accurately, and would have no reason to worry about the procedure that brought him there. Anti-Progressives, on the other hand, would be helpless to pervert the Progressive party, for the Progressive Committee is self-chosen and there is no way of attacking it except in front. To their hypocritical protests against exclusion from a share in the control, the Committee serenely says: "Take your complaint to the people! Form a rival party on any lines you like, and attract followers to your flag if you can." There could be no objection to having each substantial division of opinion among the people led by its self-appointed committee.

The followers of these leaders do not choose the leaders by intra-party elections, or formally determine where the party shall march, yet

"LEADERSHIP PARTIES" 149

despite the absence of connecting machinery they *are*, by the act of following, choosing leaders and controlling the platform. Without support the leaders are nothing, and so the leaders must cater to the voters to the utmost. In the old-style party, the leaders can often put through a nomination that is distasteful to the party membership, yet make the prestige of the party support it. But the committee in the new-style party has only the power to *invite* support. It holds no proxies. It simply says "come with us," and it can accomplish nothing unless the people come.

An old-style party is like a shop conducted on the coöperative monopoly plan, with the consumers trying to decide by vote what goods shall be carried. The consumers do not lose control of the question if they change to the competitive plan and let private shop-keepers run shops at their own risk, for the shop-keeper must carry the goods the consumers want him to carry, or fail. So in the new-style party the one essential to the success of the leaders is that they shall give the people what they want, and the control which the people thereby exercise over the party management is actually more effective than before, despite its intangibility.

We are not so very far from this even now. In many cities there are already nominating bodies, such as the rebuilt Citizens' Union in New York City, which are practically closed against invasion. The plan is the result of experience wherein the impossibility of maintaining pure reform parties has been amply demonstrated. The direct primaries have opened up new political fields, where the absence of party labels from the ballot has cleared the way for free leadership. In these primary fights real politics has appeared, in favorable contrast to the artificial, formal trumpery of so many final elections; and men have been chosen by the voters because they were "New Idea Republicans," or "La Follette men," or "Anti-Railroad," or "Local option" advocates. The people have not resented attempts at leadership, but have welcomed them and even cried out for them; and when they found a public man in whom they trusted they have forced him to speak and guide them when perhaps he would rather have kept silent.

Often the followers of a certain informal group of leaders, seeking to advance a certain idea, fight for their candidates in the primaries of both parties. The development of the primary

"LEADERSHIP PARTIES" 151

as a battle-ground will make the meaningless party divisions seem more meaningless than ever, and the next logical step will be the non-partisan primary and the non-partisan final election ballot, wiping out the strategic advantage which the machines now possess. The attitude of voters toward the "regular" nominees in the primary fights when they lack the sanctity of the party label is much more freely critical. The typical politician is usually more effective as a manipulator of machinery than as a leader of the people.

Slightly different in method, but identical in their function of leadership, are the civic organizations, which are so governed that contamination can be resisted by excluding unwelcome applicants for membership, as a social club does. These organizations, working for a principle, win outside support among the voters and their endorsement becomes valuable to candidates. It is only one step further for these organizations to foster satisfactory nominations, or even to nominate officially in their own name.

The idea of parties controlled from above instead of from below is thus not so new as it probably looked when first outlined at the beginning of this discussion.

In England the plan has been in use. In each of the parties a central self-established committee selects the candidates for each district (in England candidates need not be residents of their districts) and sends them out to campaign for the votes. The convenience and simplicity of the procedure from the standpoint of both the voters and the leaders is in its favor, and as we become more familiar with free-for-all direct-primary fights on a great scale, I think this "leadership" type of party will become increasingly common.

It is a rather essential feature of this plan that the parties shall be as free as possible to form and dissolve in the most informal fashion. They need not be, and apparently had better not be, recognized in law, or regulated except as to their expenditures. A candidate who makes so little impression on the popular consciousness that the voters need a label to identify him on the ballot, ought not to be elected at all; for such a condition implies an invisibility that is both dangerous and undemocratic. The ballots in other countries never carry any party labels. One of the best features of short ballots will undoubtedly be the fact that they can be non-partisan without

"LEADERSHIP PARTIES" 153

inconveniencing either voters or candidates, thus clearing away the old political "trust," permitting free competition, simplifying the difficulties of new parties which are now stifled at birth by the complexity of the work, and making leadership in all forms more hopeful and practicable.

CHAPTER XI

NOMINATION PROCEDURE

By an enormous mass of statutory law, American states have been attempting to introduce fair play into the myriad factional battles incident to the operation of political parties as at present organized. It was thought that if orderliness were introduced, the average American would find political details less repulsive and would take hold and see to it that the party nominees were more satisfactory. To a certain extent the hope has been justified by results. But sometimes this procedure only opened the doors wider to the easy entrance of corrupt men, and made swifter the contamination of whichever party acquired dominance. The new procedure could not make uninteresting things interesting. That the method of nominating the coroner was fair to all was not enough to make the big busy public take an interest in it, and so the remaining few who *were* interested continued to find small difficulty in having their own way. The

NOMINATION PROCEDURE

whole attempt to enable the people to protect the precious party label from capture was a very incomplete success, because the people failed to play their part according to the beautiful theory. A wiser reform would have been to make the party label less worth capturing, by shortening the final election ballot until the voters looked for the candidate instead of his label.

To plough a little deeper into the subject — the problem may be quartered according to the nature of the office, as follows: —

Nominations of —
1. Invisible officers from unwieldy districts;
2. Invisible officers from wieldy districts;
3. Visible officers from unwieldy districts;
4. Visible officers from wieldy districts.

In the first two classes, the fact that the officers are shut off from public view (by their insignificance or undebatableness of character, or by the confusion of many simultaneous contests) means that the public will have no opinion to express, and nothing is gained by the provision of better procedure for the expression of this non-existent opinion.

In the third class, direct primaries may be of great value; but they are really, in this case, simply weeding-out elections wherein the people are arbitrarily divided into two parts called respectively "Republican" and "Democratic." To have a non-partisan ballot, with all nominations made by petition, and allow the two leading candidates to appear on the ballot in the final election, would be merely a change of form, not of principle. Much evidence of the danger incident to unwieldy districts is developed in direct primary contests for governor; and candidates complain bitterly of the difficulty and expense of conducting an adequate state-wide canvass without the help of experienced ready-made vote-getting machines.

The fourth class illustrates how respect for our first two Limitations of Democracy clears away difficulties. For any procedure will suffice that will get the candidates' names on the official ballot, subject to such reasonable restriction as will exclude cranks and other candidates who have no real following. The ballot can be non-partisan, for if the office is visible the voter will not beg for a label to guide him. This dispenses with primaries and the state regulation of parties altogether, although a double election or a preferential ballot may be necessary, to prevent scattering of votes, with the corollary of a possible minority victory.

In this land of the free it does not seem likely that we can agree to print on the official ballot the name of every eligible citizen who asks to have it done, although that is the custom in parts of Canada.

Nomination by petition is a familiar expedient. The requirements vary from a mere formal handful of signatures to staggering thousands. In Des Moines, at the first election under the commission plan, where only twenty-five signatures were required to secure a place on the primary-election ballot, the number of candidates was seventy. The number will decline when the novelty of this nomination procedure wears off; but it would seem clear nevertheless that the requirements might well be increased.

In Boston, which had its first non-partisan election in 1910, five thousand signatures were required, and no voter was allowed to sign more than one petition. This prompted many voters to refuse to sign any of the petitions that happened to be offered to them. The newspapers pointed out that there was a limit to the number of candidates who would be able to get five thousand signatures in Boston without overlapping. Voters who were fearful lest some favorite of theirs would need their signature were therefore chary of signing for any one else and ended by signing for no one. As a result of these handicaps there were finally only four candidates on the ballot for mayor, although several times as many men undertook to qualify. The cost constituted the real barrier. Two of the candidates received fewer votes than the number of names on their petitions.

It is to be questioned if nomination by petition can stand the strain of regular use. It was reported in 1910 that in Los Angeles some one opened an office and conducted a business in the preparation of petitions for candidates and referenda movements, with a corps of expert canvassers to go forth and collect signatures on behalf of anybody and anything at so much a thousand. There is nothing unbelievable in the report, and its plausibility demonstrates how meaningless petitions may be. President Roosevelt once remarked to a visitor who flourished a petition in support of his request: "Petition? Petitions mean nothing!

NOMINATION PROCEDURE 159

I could get up a petition to have you hanged!" Another illustration is the success of the Independence League in getting thousands of signers for the petitions that put the names of Hearst's candidates on the official ballots of certain western counties in which the party received not a single vote in the subsequent election.

As a demonstration that a candidate has a following and is entitled to a place on the ballot for the convenience of his followers, the petition is a failure.

The petition then must be reckoned as simply an arbitrary barrier, compounded of useless labor, expense and delay, and risk of legal error, the surmounting of which indicates persistence in the candidate. Any barrier which will keep out silly candidatures would suffice and would save a lot of fruitless expenditure.

In parts of Canada and in New Zealand the candidate must make a deposit of money, fifty to two hundred dollars, as an earnest of his serious intentions, and if he fails to get a decent proportion of the votes on election day the city keeps the money as payment for having been bothered by him.

The forfeit should be as large as experience may show is necessary to exclude cranks, and no larger. The requirements will not embarrass the candidate of small means, for it need not be required of him until just long enough before the election to allow the ballot-printer to do his work. By that time the campaign will be almost closed, and the candidate will know beyond a doubt whether he is a factor in the contest. If he is afraid that he will not get the required ten or twenty per cent of the votes, the peril of forfeit will be an inducement to drop out. This will be a good thing for everybody, especially the voters, whose votes are less likely to be wasted on forlorn hopes. If he cannot satisfy some money-lender that he will get the required *minimum* of votes, he will certainly be unable to get a *plurality*. If he has real hopes of victory he will have no serious difficulty in borrowing the necessary cash for a few days, and the use of it even at usurious interest will involve far less expenditure than the getting up of a big "Notary-Publicked" petition.

Under these circumstances the real formality of nomination would occur when the candidate began to tell the neighbors of his ambitions — a prettier way of beginning than the present way of button-holing bosslets and exchanging caucus strength with candidates for other offices.

CHAPTER XII

CONCLUSION

AND now, my dear reader, we have our practical form of democracy all complete! By means of disregarding all detail and handling the elements of democracy as if they were all primitively simple and free from myriad ramifications, our imaginary reconstruction has all the fascination of the panacea. To the reader who thinks the plan really complete, I offer a restraining hand. This little book is only a sort of compass. It points to the north, but it may lead a too devout believer, not to the magnetic pole of truth, but plumb up against the wall of the house next door. It points north, but the proper route is devious and much exploration will be needed to find it.

To the reader who is sure that at some point familiar to him the proper route lies athwart my compass needle, I say: "Perhaps, and for a little while; but I have confidence that you will find yourself winding presently north

CONCLUSION

again, that permanent progress will be measured along the compass line, and that when you do find it advantageous to go to the right or left, it is because that leads to a better northward road."

I anticipate the criticism that my book is but scantily supplied with evidence, and I hasten to say that I know it. The trouble with a fact is that it is never found pure, but is always alloyed, and if I essayed to stop and note all exceptions, anticipate all misunderstandings, and measure all qualifications, this would be a ten-volume treatise and you would never read it. I am not trying to compile the evidence. If I have made you see reasonableness in these doctrines, I shall be satisfied. I have simply sketched the idea on the back of an old envelope, and the working plans must be drawn by abler architects with better equipment. I hope some day to see the book written in which these crude outlines of mine will be straightened, measured, and supplied with the needed details.

My experience with politicians in sundry little tilts I have had with them leads me to believe that to them this book, like any other discussion that takes a bird's-eye view of their profession, will be incomprehensible. I can make far easier headway with the man who is not so near the forest that the trees obscure his vision. I have found the politicians utterly unaware that there are any fundamentals underlying their existence.

Let me tell you, Mr. Politician, who you are, and what you are, and why! It will serve to the listening reader as a summing up of this volume.

You, Mr. Politician, are a unique American phenomenon! In any other democratic country you would find yourself with nothing to do. You would find that in other lands politics corresponds to the word "civics" in this country, that it concerns policies rather than political machinery, and is respectable instead of despised.

But in this country you are necessary. The designers of our governmental institutions, sitting in constitutional conventions and charter commissions, provided certain work for the people to do — and the people did n't do it. It was arranged that coroners should be selected by the people, but the people went home to bed and left the rival candidates

CONCLUSION 165

talking to a lingering handful of faithful citizens — and you, Mr. Politician, were one of the lingerers. The designers left it to the people of the state to get together and hire a man for governor, but, although there were plainly too many voters to work in unison, except by delegation of power to representatives, they provided no such method and left that work to volunteers — and you were of the volunteers.

In looking after the *neglected* work of the people, and in maintaining the machines for handling the *awkward* work, you performed needed service and deserved pay from the state. But instead of giving you definite title and salary, we made you scratch for a living in petty underpaid offices in the government, bouncing you from office with each changing administration without justice or ceremony; so your career was uncertain and precarious. Your profession, by reason of the fact that your master, the people, could not see or judge your work intelligently, was one that offered small reward to honest men (except in the few rare conspicuous offices) and big reward without danger to dishonest ones. You shared with other politicians power without responsibility. You fought the other less faithful guardians of the treasure to protect our interests, and we only damned you indiscriminately as their fellow conspirator. The damage that you permitted was as nothing to the damage you prevented.

By electing only visible officers and from wieldy districts, politics can be simplified so that the people, the candidates, and the state will perform all the work that is to be done, leaving you no function. There can be no political specialists when there is nothing to be a political specialist in! As I lay you in your grave, there passes from our American life a picturesque and original character, genial, useful, unthanked!

Of course, this is only a theoretical obituary! And, until we get a democracy that "democs," please, Mr. Politician, please stay above the sod, maintaining your wobbly oligarchy to prevent governmental chaos and collapse!

That the people have left the government to be run by politicians is creditable to the former's good sense. Imagine some less substantial electorate, such as the more mercurial population of a Latin republic, assailed with frenzied

CONCLUSION

appeals to leave business and "go into politics." They might do it, to the utter demoralization of industry prior to each election. And we should say: "How deplorable! What a bad sense of proportion they show in fussing with caucuses and rallies when they ought to be ploughing the fields and caring for their families!" Of the enthusiastic volunteer we should say: "The time he devotes to unpaid work in politics could better be used in paid work at his business, so that he could give his children a better schooling or his wife a new hat"; and we should be right. It is because they *are* doing their duty that the American people do not go into politics. Duty to the family outweighs duty to the state.

Yet in no way is this rightly to be construed as applause for civic laziness. It is not a justification of the man who thinks only of his own affairs and ignores those of the community. We are getting rather away from such narrow selfishness. We talk of "conservation of national resources," "regulation of the labor of women and children," "the prevention of tuberculosis"—these things are our real politics. The citizen does have duties in such directions.

But "peanut politics," that unique American

institution, is a different matter. It is not the people's paramount duty to fret over whether Jones or Smith shall be made a delegate to a convention to nominate a candidate for a petty aldermanic post, or whether the Brown faction or the Robinson crowd shall control the patronage of the county clerk's office. "Taking an interest in politics" ought to mean something bigger than hanging around political headquarters, or learning the names of the county committee, or getting up chowder-parties. The citizen owes no duty to "peanut politics" except to get it abolished in favor of the big "common welfare" kind of politics that lies beyond.

What good sense the American people have shown in silently ignoring "peanut politics" and refusing to believe that the privilege of electing the register of deeds was the kind of liberty the Pilgrim fathers crossed the sea for! A people who stick resolutely to their firesides and their work, — yes, to money-making, — and stubbornly wait for politics to come to them, are showing a sober, instinctive common sense that is sounder than the logic of those who scold them.

I promised in the first chapter to land you

CONCLUSION

here free of cynicism regarding our people in politics, and possessed of a belief that, with like mechanisms of expression, they would prove themselves as good as the people of those foreign democracies where good government seems normal.

Have I succeeded?

L'ENVOI

WELL, my friend reader, what shall we do about it? Shall the book go on the shelf and be classed as the academic proposal of a dreamer? Or is it to be a flag to follow?

I've started already.

In this year, 1911, certain things are beginning that you, as a reader of this little volume, this year or later, should know of. The Short-Ballot Organization has been formed to explain the Short-Ballot principle to the American people.

The President is WOODROW WILSON, of Princeton, N. J.

The Vice-Presidents are: —
  WINSTON CHURCHILL, Cornish, N. H.
  HORACE E. DEMING, New York, N. Y.
  BEN B. LINDSEY, Denver, Colo.
  WILLIAM S. U'REN, Oregon City, Ore.
  WILLIAM ALLEN WHITE, Emporia, Kan.
  CLINTON ROGERS WOODRUFF, Philadelphia, Pa.

The Advisory Board are: —
  LAWRENCE F. ABBOTT, New York, N. Y.

HENRY JONES FORD, Princeton, N. J.
RICHARD S. CHILDS, New York City.
NORMAN HAPGOOD, New York City.
WOODROW WILSON, Princeton, N. J.

The author is Secretary, with offices at 383 Fourth Avenue, New York.

Provision is made for the enrollment in our list of "Short-Ballot Advocates" of any one who believes in the Short-Ballot principle. No dues or duties. Enrolled advocates — there are twelve thousand of them now — receive occasional bulletins of opportunities to help, and to them our publications are free.

We have been organized only a year at this writing, but we have seeded the country with pamphlets and publicity — and we are beginning to reap already.

Are you with us?

The Riverside Press
CAMBRIDGE · MASSACHUSETTS
U . S . A